FAITH
and
YOU

· VOLUME 2 ·

Also by Terry Pluto

On faith and other topics:

Faith and You
Everyday Faith
Champions for Life: The Power of a Father's Blessing (with Bill Glass)
Crime: Our Second Vietnam (with Bill Glass)

On sports:

Joe Tait: It's Been a Real Ball
Things I've Learned from Watching the Browns
LeBron James: The Making of an MVP (with Brian Windhorst)
The Franchise (with Brian Windhorst)
Dealing: The Cleveland Indians' New Ballgame
False Start: How the New Browns Were Set Up to Fail
The View from Pluto
Unguarded (with Lenny Wilkens)
Our Tribe
Browns Town 1964
Burying the Curse
The Curse of Rocky Colavito
Falling from Grace
Tall Tales
Loose Balls
Bull Session (with Johnny Kerr)
Tark (with Jerry Tarkanian)
Forty-Eight Minutes, a Night in the Life of the NBA (with Bob Ryan)
Sixty-One (with Tony Kubek)
You Could Argue But You'd Be Wrong (with Pete Franklin)
Weaver on Strategy (with Earl Weaver)
The Earl of Baltimore
Super Joe (with Joe Charboneau and Burt Graeff)
The Greatest Summer

FAITH
and
YOU

• VOLUME 2 •

More Essays on Faith
in Everyday Life

Terry Pluto

GRAY & COMPANY, PUBLISHERS
CLEVELAND

A portion of the royalties from this book will be given to The Haven of Rest, Akron's city mission.

Gray & Company, Publishers
www.grayco.com

ISBN: 978-1-938441-12-7
Printed in the United States of America

1

To my wife Roberta, God's greatest gift to me.
I married on a major upgrade!

Contents

Introduction

My faith column didn't start as a faith column.

The year was 2000. I was working for the *Akron Beacon Journal*. So was Regina Brett, until the *Plain Dealer* in Cleveland hired her.

Yes, the same *Plain Dealer* where I worked as a baseball writer from late 1979 to 1984. And, yes, the same *Plain Dealer* where I returned in 2007. It's where my faith column—Faith and You—is published twice a month.

But the faith column began at the *Akron Beacon Journal* in 2000 because the *Plain Dealer* had hired away Brett. Jan Leach was the *Beacon Journal's* editor. She asked if I was interested in switching from sports to Brett's old job as a general columnist.

I had never seen that change work, especially when a person has been writing about sports for decades. For better or worse, I was a "sports guy." And for me, that was best, because I like and understand sports.

With sports, when in doubt, go to a game. You have a winner and a loser. You often have conflict. Write about the Browns, and you have an instant audience across the country because so many people love to read almost anything about the guys in the orange helmets.

When I said "no," that led to a conversation about other things, including the weekly jail ministry that I was doing.

I told Leach about one of the first times I was in a prison. I was with Bill Glass, the former Browns star defensive end who has spent more than 40 years in prison ministry. We were in a Texas prison when a skinhead-type inmate approached me. He had several teardrop tattoos under both eyes. You don't get those for attending Rotary Club meetings or volunteering to read books at the local senior citizens home.

"You're new, right?" the guy asked.

I said that was true.

"You scared?" he asked.

"A bit," I said.

"Don't worry about it," he said. "You guys who come in as volunteers . . . anyone in here touches you, we'll kill 'em!"

He laughed.

I smiled, sort of.

"I ain't joking," he said.

He then explained how it works in most prisons and jails. Those who teach Bible or art or GED classes—or do about anything to help inmates—are considered an exalted class of people.

"Even if you don't care about the Bible or art, you don't mess with them," he said. "But the deputies and other staff people, it's a different story. That's not you, so don't worry about it."

That scouting report has turned out to be true.

My editor, Leach, seemed fascinated.

I told her about an inmate who showed me a huge burn mark on his chest. When he was young, his mother put it there . . . with a hot iron. There were tears in his eyes as he recalled the story. The guy was at least 40.

I told her about a guy who worked in the payroll department of a major airline. He created an extra account for himself in which a vice president's salary was sent directly to a bank. One night at a party, he got drunk and bragged about it. He had made more than $100,000 with this scam. A friend asked if the guy could cut him a $5,000 check to buy a car. The man did.

"Really dumb," the inmate told me.

It got worse. The friend took the check to the bank drive-through window. That's right: he wanted $5,000 cash at the drive-through window.

Naturally, the teller asked the friend to come inside. The friend panicked and drove off.

And, yes, he left the check with the teller, who didn't have to graduate from Quantico to figure out something was wrong. The bank called the airline, which traced the check to the guy in the payroll department. That led to five years on a plea deal.

"For most of these guys, greed gets them every time," I said.

My editor wanted to hear more stories.

I told her about how nearly everyone in prison has a "father problem." Dad was abusive. Dad was missing. Dad was addicted. Dad was anything but a dad.

I did mention what I call the "90-10" rule. In 90 percent of the cases, you don't have to look far to find the source of the problems.

"Family mess." That's what my friend Bishop Joey Johnson of Akron House of the Lord calls it.

But in the other 10 percent, the families were solid—the inmate just wanted to do dumb stuff and was so selfish, he didn't care if he got caught. I run into those parents and I tell them, "It's not your fault."

And it's not.

Some people just insist on doing life "their way," which also is the hard way. And that translates into some hard time.

That led to a discussion about faith writing in the paper, where Jim Carney did an excellent job covering the local religious scene. But the *Beacon Journal* was publishing syndicated columns.

"Those have absolutely nothing to do with faith," I said.

"What do you mean?" Leach asked.

I explained how they were "about denominational spitball fights, this group of Methodists is mad at that group of Methodists, etc."

They were about gay bishops.

They were about abortion.

They were about the death penalty.

They were about gay marriage.

They were about the issue of separation of church and state.

They were about scandals in various churches.

They were not about things that most people of faith—or even those not especially interested in faith—faced each day.

"What would you write about?" Leach asked.

"I'd start with what I won't write about," I said. "It's the list of political hot-button issues that have moved into the faith arena. There are thousands of words written on those subjects each day. I have nothing to add on stuff like abortion, gay rights or the death penalty.

"In fact, in jail ministry, you learn these words: 'I have no opinion on the death penalty.' That's because even if you do, you don't say it. Not if you want to continue to minister to men who may be facing the death penalty, or work with people in a system where the death penalty is in place."

Leach seemed to understand.

"Besides, I have nothing new to say about that subject," I said.

She asked again, "What would you write about?"

"How it feels when your prayers aren't answered," I said. "Or how you can be a person of faith but be so overwhelmed by what's happening that you can't pray."

In Romans 8:26, the apostle Paul writes, "The Spirit helps us in our weakness. We do not know what we ought to pray for, but the Spirit intercedes for us with groans that words cannot express."

One of my goals is to write about people struggling with faith, or people in pain—physical or emotional.

I told her: "Far more people are dealing with what I did when my father had a major stroke and was disabled and unable to speak for almost five years than there are people who deal with the political hot-button issues. But we rarely write about the personal side of faith."

Leach seemed interested and said we'd talk more.

I heard nothing for almost six months, so I assumed the idea was dead.

Then Leach asked me to write two sample columns. The first was about unanswered prayers, or at least prayers not answered as we had hoped. The second was about dealing with the issues of elder care. Leach read them and decided to publish them.

"Can you write two or three a month?" she asked.

I took it both as a challenge and as God opening a door for the type of writing seldom found in a major mainstream newspaper. Journalists are bold enough to write about almost any lifestyle, any diet and any way to buy a car, use a credit card or pick a gas company, but they grow silent on faith, at least the personal type.

At first there were a few complaints about the column, with some readers making the "separation of church and state" argument. But because I did not represent a church, and the state or government did not own or sponsor the paper, that argument was weak.

I still receive a few emails each year asking, "Why are you writing about God on the religion page?"

Think about that for a moment. The answer is obvious. As I often reply, "It's sort of like writing about the Browns on the sports page—God . . . the religion page . . . don't you think that fits?"

After several months the strength of the column became what was first perceived to be one of its weaknesses: Its author is a sportswriter, not a theological or ordained minister.

Yes, I lead a jail Bible class and weekly service, but that hardly makes me a full-time member of the clergy. And while I come from the Judeo-Christian perspective, my goal is not to convert anyone reading the paper. It is to make them think, and also to bring some comfort to those in emotional struggles with God or life. I write about the times when I act like a jerk, when I stuff my faith in my back pocket and then forget about it as I sit on it.

I write for people who need to hear this from Psalm 34:18:

"The Lord is close to the brokenhearted and saves those who are crushed in spirit."

That's because so many of us go through periods where we feel like that: "brokenhearted . . . crushed in spirit."

My job is to give those people a voice, and to talk about the kind of faith we need to get through what life throws at us each day.

FAITH IN WHAT?

You said what many parents needed to hear. Thanks for an article that I will pass on to my children for advice I may not be here to give them.

—Peg Healy, North Ridgeville

- 1 -

Kneeling at the Altar of Sports

I received this email from Mark right after LeBron James won
the 2012 NBA title with the Miami Heat:

> I lost my faith in sports. It hurt to the core. This isn't about
> LeBron leaving Cleveland, but the disrespect Miami showed for
> the game of basketball. I love this game. There's nothing like
> the feeling of swishing a three with a hand in your face. It's a
> great game. But seeing the Heat win has just taken away any
> respect and faith I had for the game at the highest level. The
> Heat reminded me of a spoiled brat who whined and cried when
> he didn't get his way.
>
> They complained about the refs, both during and after the
> game. They taunted opponents. . . . The stupid celebration/wel-
> come party they had before they had won anything. . . . LeBron
> finally hit some clutch free throws, but the way Dwayne Wade
> and LeBron and the rest act takes away from that. And then for
> them to be rewarded for their behavior with a championship? It's
> just hard to watch. There's no respect for their opponents. There's
> no respect for the game. There's no respect for those who made
> this game great. It's all about them getting their way. What kind
> of message does this send? . . .
>
> I grew up a Cleveland fan. Naturally, I'm emotionally invested

in sports. I'm passionate about it to the point where the frustration is tough to handle. The hits keep on coming, and we keep getting bashed by those outside our city limits. And I'm sad to say, this will bring more negative light to a city down on its luck having trouble getting and keeping players.

Over the years some of us have allowed our identity as a people and a place to be intertwined with the sports teams.

If the Indians, Browns or Cavs are doing well . . . then so is Cleveland.

If not, then there must be something wrong with us.

As Mark also wrote:

> As a Cleveland fan, we get ripped on a lot. Told we will never amount to anything, never be relevant. Never win it all. I really want the best for the city I come from. I have so much pride and appreciation for the things we do contribute (Cleveland Clinic, the arts, culinary, etc.) and for the people that live here. I'm sick of the naysayers and hearing the celebrations from anyone else's camp. I want to see us hoist that trophy and just take in the moment. This hardworking town with great people will have something to celebrate.

Just reading that, you know Mark is off-track.

Mark knows it, too.

"Unfortunately, I've attached sports to real life," he confessed.

When the Browns moved to Baltimore, did downtown Cleveland just fall into Lake Erie? Did all the people lose their jobs? Was Northeast Ohio hit with a case of the plague?

Really, what happened, other than football fans had to find something else to do on fall Sunday afternoons?

And they had to find something else to talk about, besides who should play quarterback or coach the team in the orange helmets?

I'm a sportswriter. I'm thankful that Cleveland has three

Major League teams because they do give me something to write and talk about.

But should we allow our loyalty to the teams and our longing for their success to in any way define us?

Mark struggles with that, as he wrote:

> I'm starting to lose the point of being a sports fan when it just brings so much frustration and rewards to those who don't make it worth watching. Worst of all, I'm letting something like that affect my mood. All those great moments of history seem less great when those who took the easy way out will be remembered as 'champions.' There's plenty of so-called 'champions' that I don't believe should have the title. To me, sports should build character, and we are getting away from that.

Too many of us have turned professional sports into an idol. For some football fans, Sunday's High Church is a tailgate party starting at 6 a.m. For more than a few of us, our attitude is shaped by how our favorite teams performed.

And if we take a moment to think about it, we know that doesn't make much sense.

*   *   *

There's the myth of sports and the reality.

The myth is if you work hard enough, prepare wisely and don't drink, smoke, chew or hang around with those who do, well, in the end, you will win more than you lose.

But the fact is lots of people "win" in certain parts of life who seem not to "deserve" it. Some took shortcuts. Some flat-out cheated. I know dedicated, fanatical athletes who worked out constantly and hated to even take an aspirin for pain—yet they didn't perform as well as some guys who played through hangovers, smoked dope and hated to lift weights.

Or as we in the media sometimes say when being around certain athletes, "That guy makes it in spite of himself."

That's because the athlete is blessed with such overwhelming natural talent, it almost doesn't matter what he does—as long as he shows up for practices and games.

Meanwhile, lots of good people who do the right things don't win in the end, or at least it seems that way.

When I talk to groups of people and young athletes, they often want me to say, "You can do anything you want to do in life."

Really? Anything?

Let's start with the fact that 99.9 percent of the population has no chance of ever playing center in the NBA, because they aren't or won't be tall enough. Or they won't play on the line in the NFL because they aren't big enough, as 300 pounds is the norm.

But when it comes to sports, it's more than a matter of height and weight.

If you can't throw a baseball at least 90 mph—and 99 percent of the population will never be able to do so—you have almost zero chance of being signed to a professional pitching contract. Some pitchers reach the Major Leagues who don't throw that hard, but nearly all of them were at 90 mph at some point in their careers.

I've spent most of my life around elite athletes, and they are in the top five percent of the gene pool. Even rather ordinary looking athletes in terms of size often have extraordinary hand-eye coordination, foot speed or vision.

When Mike Hargrove played for the Indians, he was a rather normal appearing 6-foot, 200-pounder. He didn't run especially fast. One day I was talking with him—and a fly was buzzing us. He looked at it for a few seconds, then grabbed it right out of the air. Caught it in his bare hand.

That's why he could hit a 95-mph fastball that looked mostly like a white blur to us.

And even in the top five percent of the gene pool, there are differences. Some are in the top one percent, such as LeBron

James. He was an All-State football player, and I had major college coaches and former pro assistants tell me that James could have been a star in the NFL.

To most physically blessed athletes, almost any sport comes shockingly easy to them—at least in terms of them playing it at an acceptable level, higher than most of us dream.

But that they are physically blessed doesn't make them smart, even if their intelligence is above average.

Proverbs 16:16 reads: "How much better to get wisdom than gold."

Proverbs 3:13 reads: "Blessed is the man who finds wisdom, the man who gains understanding."

There's a huge difference between being smart and being wise.

The Bible also talks about wisdom coming from "the fear of the Lord." And that fear of the Lord is about respecting God and others.

But sports is about beating the other guy . . . and in modern times, bragging about it. Talk trash, pound your chest, strut around, loom large in the spotlight already on you.

Very little about big-time sports has much to do with real life, at least when the athletes are on top.

Later, poor decisions and arrogance catch up with most of them. All the millions are gone, the friends leave, and divorces and lawsuits arrive.

And no one cares that once upon a time you used to be a pretty good linebacker or second baseman.

One of the saddest figures is the frustrated former athlete talking about "What used to be" and/or "What could have been."

When I was young, I dreamed of becoming a professional baseball player.

By junior high I knew it would never happen. Not at 5-foot-9, 115 pounds with glasses, poor hand-eye coordination and a father who was a former minor-league baseball player. We often were around top amateur players as my older brother was a successful high school coach. Physically, I knew that I could never come close to matching them. Even though I was on excellent high school baseball teams and played one year of small college ball, I knew my limitations and was planning for real life.

And I'm thankful for that, because even the best athletes in the world reach their late 30s and have to ask, "What do I do now?"

That's because time does catch up with them—and real life scares them.

And that's something seldom mentioned when talking to young athletes and their parents. Like all dreams, even being a millionaire athlete has its dark side.

*   *   *

Mark also wrote:

A lot of frustration on my part is knowing this doesn't mean the world. It's not life, yet it still bugs me. I believe it to be silly, yet the frustration mounts. I love sports. I love competition. I love the games. Sports helped shape me into the hard-working, passionate person I am today. When I played as a kid, I left everything on the field, every single game. Now I have a job I truly enjoy. I'm quickly gaining more responsibility. I exhaust my effort every day to do the best that I can do. Unfortunately, sports have not been the distraction from life I'd like it to be . . . I think this is because I've taken it too personally.

However, Mark took the best from sports—the concepts of teamwork, dedication, bouncing back from defeat, and a willingness to take instruction and be coached—and applied that to real life.

Part of the reason that amateur sports may be more important than ever is we have a large number of boys growing up without men in the house. Coaches serve as men, telling them what to do. They set standards and tolerate few excuses. Athletes often call them "father figures" because they are the closest thing to a father. A great coach in high school or elsewhere in the amateur ranks is worth far more than a millionaire coach in the pros.

That's also true for young women, many of whom also lack fathers in the home. Most girls' sports are coached by men—or a combination of men and women. Or if it's just female coaches, they still serve as another voice of authority besides Mom at home.

Mark wrote:

> I guess I just want to find a way to enjoy the sports I love so much again. . . . I want to find that perspective so I take sports for what they are worth, a diversion from our real-life issues. I want to find the balance between passionate and frustrated. After all, isn't it just a game?

The real value of pro sports is evident when family members go to games . . . and then think back about those times years later. How many of us remember the scores, or even who won? That we were at the games with someone who cared about us mattered most.

Amanda Rabinowitz is a newscaster for National Public Radio. Her father died when she was 16. One of her best memories is how her father would take her to New York Mets games. Old Shea Stadium was a dump. The Mets weren't very good. Her father battled cancer for the final 10 years of his life—but he made a point of taking her to those games. She now works in Northeast Ohio and has become a Tribe fan. Whenever she goes to an Indians game, she thinks of her dad.

She fights back the tears when talking about how her father would play catch with her. She knew she was bugging him, and she knew he was tired. But outside they'd go, and throw the ball back and forth. Only as an adult did she realize how much pain he endured in those games of catch because he cared more about his daughter than what cancer was doing to him at that moment.

When my father was suffering from a stroke and couldn't go

to games, or talk, or even leave the house, he still loved to watch the games on television. He preferred his teams to win, but if not ... just having the game to help get him through that night was what mattered the most.

And it also mattered to me, because those games made those nights better for us.

When LeBron James left the Cavs to sign with Miami, I received several emails from fans who acted as if this was one of the worst things that could happen to the city, the Cavs and, yes, even to them.

To a few, I wrote back: "If LeBron leaving is the worst thing that happens to you this month, sign up for it right now."

Anyone who has ever received a doctor's report about cancer or blockage in the heart or a disease they can't quite figure out how to treat ... well, we know where sports really belong on our list of priorities.

Or when a job leaves town, compared with the Browns leaving.

Or when a car breaks down ...

Or a parent dies ...

Or a friendship falls apart ...

Or ...

We can spend a lot of time making a list of what really matters before coming up with, "The Indians winning the World Series" or "The Browns winning a Super Bowl."

When we are faced with a real problem, we don't pray to LeBron James or the memory of Paul Brown.

Many of us tend to follow Psalm 121, which starts:

"I lift up my eyes to the hills—
Where does my help come from?
My help comes from the Lord,
The Maker of heaven and earth."

- 2 -

Who Are We . . . Working For?

When I became serious about my faith in 1997, I had a problem.

As the sports columnist for the *Akron Beacon Journal*, my job was to write opinions, and some of those opinions were critical.

Is that what a faithful person should do?

I once wrote a column that began: "Art Modell looked as if he had just passed some very bad gas."

That story—about the day the former Cleveland Browns owner publicly signed the deal that moved the franchise to Baltimore—ended up winning an award.

At the time I was rather far from God and not especially concerned with treating sports scoundrels such as Modell with much fairness.

I once wrote that a Tribe pitcher "wasn't the brightest bulb on any stadium light pole." The young pitcher departed after the season ended in September and left his final paycheck—about $5,000—in his locker at the stadium. In the spring the guys who clean the clubhouse discovered the check. The pitcher apparently never noticed the missing cash, his final two weeks of salary.

I'm not especially proud of either story now, although both were popular with readers.

How was I supposed to handle stories such as these? How was

I supposed to show my faith at work?

I've heard pastors suggest that people start Bible studies, or get together for prayer and other activities at lunch.

"But the real answer is simply do your job well," said Mike Castelli, a pastor at The Chapel in Akron since 2000. Before that he was a research engineer at NASA for a dozen years.

"Actions speak louder than words," Castelli said. "Not everyone can be a star on their job, but everyone can do their job with integrity and be accountable."

How does integrity play into my job?

If I were to write with integrity, would I have to ignore the duplicity and deceit of Modell and others when they moved the Browns? Or would I look the other way when a team made a series of lousy trades?

At the time I talked with two pastors who had been public figures for a long time but who didn't seem like wimpy "church guys." Close friends, they ran large churches in Akron. Knute Larson was from The Chapel, primarily a white church. Ronald Fowler was from the Arlington Church of God, mostly a black church.

I spoke to them separately, and both gave me the same advice: Of course, I must be critical in my job when the situation demanded it. But they also said: Criticize the action, not the person.

A guy can make a bad trade but that doesn't make him an idiot.

Be critical of Modell's business practices, but keep personal cheap shots out of the story.

They also asked me if, when writing, was I looking for reasons to be negative? Or was I looking to be fair?

After all, negative tends to draw more attention from fans and readers.

But that doesn't make it right.

* * *

It's an attitude issue, one we all face no matter where we work.

"There can be a lot of anger and resentment on the job," said Rev. Bill Buckeye, pastor of Bay United Methodist Church in Bay Village. "It's so easy to look around and think, 'I'm doing more work than that other person.'"

The fact is that some bosses are jerks and should not have been promoted. Some people work less and receive more pay and praise.

But Rev. Buckeye said we should not pour our ragged emotions and hurt feelings on people all day. We're not paid to do that.

Proverbs 14:30 reads: "A heart at peace gives life to the body, but envy rots the bones."

How many of us look around and say, "That lady over there makes less than I do and she does a better job than I do."

Instead, we mentally seek out the slacker, someone who by comparison makes us look good at work.

Do we allow frustrations at our job to affect how we do our work? Is it fair if I'm having a bad day with a boss to unload in a story on a quarterback who has a rough day on the field?

When I go to work, what is my mindset? Am I mad at my boss or my co-workers even before I begin the job?

My friend Bill Glass is a former Browns defensive end who has spent more than 40 years in prison ministry. We were talking about my job, and he said, "When I'm not sure if I should go positive or negative in a situation or conversation, I go positive."

"Why?" I asked.

"Because I can always go negative later," he said. "But if I'm unsure, and go negative, and turn out to be wrong, then I'm in a bad spot with that person. Waiting can clarify most things."

But I'm in a business that demands an instant opinion, or "take" as it's now called.

Sometimes I don't know what to say.

For example, an assistant coach is hired to be the head coach.

It's almost impossible to guess how he will perform because he has no track record or experience in that job. Being an assistant can be excellent preparation, but it's not an indication of what will happen.

I frustrate some readers when I'm not overly critical of a new coach or general manager. I tend to take the Bill Glass approach, unless the guy has a horrible track record.

Give the guy a chance. Treat him as you'd like to be treated as you begin a job. Can we at least let him lose some preseason games before we write him off?

While most people have a different job than I, the same principle applies. A new boss is hired. Do I give the person a chance, or do I look for reasons to go negative?

I've heard media people react harshly when a new coach is hired. Then they nitpick the guy just to prove their opinion is right. Validating their view becomes far more important than explaining what really is taking place.

A young writer was covering a major college team that hired a coach who had NCAA problems in his past. She called to talk about how to handle the story. I told her to discuss those issues, but pay as much attention to how the school thought this guy would stay out of trouble in his new job. And, I said, let the coach explain what he learned from his past as it applied to what he planned to do.

"Besides," I told her, "if he hasn't changed, it will come up soon enough. The NCAA is watching him closely. Give him a chance to fail without assuming he will."

Within two years the coach had violated more NCAA rules.

I still think it was right to give the coach the benefit of the doubt as he started his new job.

* * *

Some people believe the way to show their faith at work is to act as if they're the office pastor or rabbi. Many employers have stories about the person who has a big Bible at his or her desk but is chronically late, or whose work is inconsistent.

"When you first get to know people at work, they don't want you to tell them about your faith," said R. A. Vernon, pastor of The Word Church based in Warrensville Heights. "They want to see it. If you spend your work time on Facebook or surfing the Internet, they notice. If you steal paper and things, they notice. Your boss does not pay you to pray and preach on his time. Do it on your break or after work."

Doing a good job means working hard to meet deadlines and refusing to make promises that can't be kept. We should let someone know if we will be late, and quickly apologize when we're wrong, instead of offering a list of excuses.

In Matthew 5:37, Jesus said: "Simply let your 'Yes' be 'Yes,' and your 'No,' 'No.'"

People need to be able to count on us to keep our word. And we must be willing to tell someone "No" when we know it's not the answer that person wants. Our goal is not to be liked but to be respected for our integrity.

Vernon mentioned Colossians 3:23: "Whatever you do, work at it with all your heart as [if] working for the Lord, not for men."

Then he told this story: "I worked construction. I was in the union and I encountered some racism because some people thought I didn't deserve the job that I had. It was tough. But I still had to show them respect, even if they didn't always earn it."

Pastor David Loar from the Fairlawn United Church of Christ once worked in a foundry cleaning up. Loar said a co-worker, a man of faith, impressed him "because he really kept his area clean so others didn't have to clean up after him."

The Chapel's Castelli cited this quote from German theologian Martin Luther: "The maid who sweeps her kitchen is doing the will of God just as much as the monk who prays—not because she may sing a Christian hymn as she sweeps but because God loves clean floors."

Bishop Joey Johnson of Akron's House of the Lord talked

about working in places where people who insisted they were Christians took 45 minutes for a 15-minute break. They gossiped. They sought attention.

But we are not paid to blend into the mediocre middle. Neither should we complain more or gossip to fit in.

"The way to get people interested in your faith is to do your job well and quietly, not caring who gets the credit or the promotion," said Joe Coffey, pastor of Christ Community Church in Hudson.

It is hard not to fall through the trapdoor of office politics. At some point everyone will be hurt and slighted on the job. How do we handle it? One friend of mine goes to the ladies' room to say a quick prayer, take a few deep breaths and pull herself together.

This does not mean we should accept sexual or physical harassment on the job or that we live with a boss who unleashes constant verbal abuse. But we should treat co-workers and bosses with grace and patience, especially when they are having a bad day.

Jesus did say in Luke 6:31: "Do to others as you would have them do to you."

"Adversity is part of work," Vernon said. "Some is the drama and dealing with people who have lots of issues."

Or as Arlington Church of God worship leader Leslie Parker Barnes often says: "Just about everyone has something big going on in their lives."

That may explain why someone seems to be acting out of character. We should keep in mind that the way we interact with those people and others in the workplace can demonstrate our faith.

"If we treat people well, then some people will want to talk to us about their problems," Vernon said. "They will be interested in our faith and we'll begin to read the Bible with them on a break. But first we must do our job well."

3

Yes, Church Does Matter

I go to church nearly every Sunday, whether I'm at home or on the road. If not on Sunday, I try to find a Saturday night service.

Some people say, "I can be close to God walking in the woods or quietly spending an hour in my chair reading the Bible and praying."

That may be true, but how many of us actually take the time to do that?

When I want to hear from God, I sometimes take a four-mile hike in the Cuyahoga Valley National Park. Being away from computers, my cell phone and other distractions allows me to think about a lot of things—and talk with God.

Psalm 46:10 reads: "Be still and know I am God."

The truth is that most people don't go to park or even sit quietly and try to connect with God.

When Sunday comes, they sleep in. They golf. They answer emails and update Facebook and Twitter. Most of us skip church because we don't feel like going. We think the pastor is boring, the people are phonies and we're tired.

What good is it to have a Sabbath if you don't get to sleep in, right?

How can this change?

Start with the 10-minute rule.

Ten-minute rule?

Some people are only willing to attend a church that is within 10 minutes of their house. I was one of those people until years ago when a friend asked me how far I drive to see a game or even get to my favorite pizza place. It was much longer than a 10-minute trip.

I have a friend who is a pastor in India. He talks about people walking 10 miles to his church. Priests who served in Latin America have told me similar stories. A priest told me about his first Mass in El Salvador. His sermon lasted about 15 minutes, longer than the usual 10 that he spoke in the United States. The service lasted about an hour. He was afraid people would think it was too long.

Instead, some people stayed in church after it was over. Others went outside and began setting up for what became a church lunch.

When the eating was over, they wanted to have a prayer and healing service. And more singing. With another sermon, sort of a Bible study.

My friend in India does the same . . . he says a Mass, then there's lunch. Then there's prayer, praise and teaching. These people don't have computers. They treasure the Bible and any other religious books that he has to give them.

Every few years my friend from India comes to America and says Mass at a few churches here, while also raising money for his mission that cares for orphans and widows.

He notices that a few minutes into his sermon, Americans begin looking at their watches. Not all of the people in the pews, but enough for him to notice.

For years, I was no different. When I went to church, I wanted a short sermon, a quick service and get this thing over. I acted as if I was going for an outpatient procedure at a hospital.

We take for granted everything from clean water to heated homes to an incredible variety of food at grocery stores. Our basic needs (not wants) can be met by various social agencies. We also are blessed with an incredible variety of ways and places to worship.

But so many of us don't even bother to look.

If some of us worked as hard to find the right church as we do to find a car, find a date or find something that is important to us, we'd probably find a church where we can make a connection.

* * *

At this point you may be saying, "Who is Terry Pluto to tell me to go to church?"

Well, these are stories about faith. Each week in The *Plain Dealer*, our health section publishes stories about the need for exercise and the best workouts. We share information about diets and what we should eat to be healthy. On the business pages are stories about how best to handle money. Other sections have stories about the best cars to buy, the top movies and plays to watch.

Go to any bookstore and there are so many books telling us how best to live our lives.

My point is that if we are serious about faith, we should be at a place where others share the same interest. I thought of that while reading a report from George Barna, a respected pollster when it comes to faith issues. His research revealed that about 80 percent of people identify themselves as "Christians" but only 47 percent regularly attend church.

More revealing, 31 percent admitted that they had not been to church in the past six months unless it was to a wedding or a funeral.

Among people who said they were Catholic, weekly attendance was 49 percent. For "born again" Christians, it was 59 percent. For those in the general Protestant category, it was under 50 percent.

There are times, of course, when everyone misses church for a good reason. But to grow in faith, church is essential. Just as most of us know that we exercise harder if we go to a gym and make even more progress if we join a class at the health club.

It's easy to say, "I don't need someone preaching at me."

But I do need someone reminding me about the dangers of gossip, about the need to be more patient with others around me. I know these things, but I still need to hear them—along with so much more.

A good church or any other house of worship (notice that I didn't say a "perfect" church or house of worship) is a place for that, and more.

But we have to ask ourselves if we are willing to make the effort to find one.

*   *   *

All places of worship are not created equal.

Some people sound like fussy shoppers, though, concerned only about what the church should give them.

Yes, it makes sense for a young family to find a church with a good children's ministry and youth program. For those who can't drive, it's wise to find a church that supplies transportation for people who need it. Some churches are strong in music and the arts; others have sports and outdoor activities.

But it works both ways: We also serve the church. My wife and I drive separately each Sunday because we take three to five people without cars to church. It helps us to connect with them, and the rides become part of the church service.

Over the years I have received a few emails about skipping church, "because it's filled with phonies and hypocrites."

"It's true, there are phonies in churches," said Scott Wilson, pastor of Mayfield United Methodist Church in Chesterland. "And most of us should fit right in."

Wilson explained that his point is: "We are all human beings, and we all can be selfish and sinners. Church is a good place to work on that."

By their nature, churches are messy.

In Matthew 9:11-13, some in the religious establishment ask why Jesus eats "with tax collectors and sinners."

Jesus said: "It is not the healthy who need a doctor, but the sick. But go and learn what this means: 'I desire mercy, not sacrifice.' For I have not come to call the righteous, but sinners."

Most churches say they want anyone to come in. "Anyone" means anyone from old to young, from conservatives to liberals, from those having emotional struggles to someone being harshly judgmental.

No one checks criminal records, administers intelligence tests or checks for spiritual maturity at the door. There are no requirements that anyone even be emotionally balanced. Anyone means just that . . . anyone.

If you're an adult, no one even forces you to go.

"Our main reason for going to church should not be horizontal," said Paul Sartarelli, pastor of The Chapel in Akron. "It shouldn't be all about the other people in church. Our main goal should be vertical—to connect with God. Of course, we want to connect horizontally—with the people around us. But it's our relationship with God that comes first."

Sartarelli said that once we give a church a chance and "get to know some people, we also may be more understanding of them. We will find they are dealing with some real challenges in their lives. And, hopefully, they can help us with what we are facing."

Eventually, you will probably hear the story of the choir director sleeping with a Sunday school teacher—while each is married to someone else.

Or the pastor who dumps his wife for a younger woman.

Or the seemingly demure middle-aged woman who was skimming cash from the collection plates.

"I understand that people have been hurt by churches," said

Roger Gries, auxiliary bishop of the Catholic Diocese of Cleveland. "I deal with the anger because of the scandals in the Catholic Church. It's real. We must not run from it. But it's also a fact that more than 95 percent of priests and bishops have been pointing people toward God, toward salvation and trying to help us all improve our lives by living it the right way."

It's also easier to look at the faults of others than to stare into the mirror of your own soul.

I've unleashed the Inner Jerk in me when someone asked me for a favor while I was tired or distracted. That has led some people to rightly say, "And he calls himself a follower of God?"

Donnie McClurkin wrote a gospel song called "We Fall Down." Its chorus is, "We fall down, but we get up. For a saint is just a sinner who fell down and got up."

That is also true for people in church.

4

Why Work Matters

A friend asked me to speak to students at a local broadcasting school.

I know nothing about jobs in radio and television. OK, I know something. I know that whenever I've been a guest on network television shows, they always want to put a lot of powder on my bald head to "cut down on the glare."

I could have suggested to the students that they don't lose their hair—and if they do, to make sure to find a good wig that doesn't look as if a small animal had died on top of their head.

But I don't think that's what they had in mind.

So I spent five minutes asking God, "What do these people need to hear?"

I wasn't hit by any lightning bolts. No stone tablets were handed to me. I did think of Proverbs 10:19: "When words are many, sin is not absent, but he who holds his tongue is wise."

Those are not exactly inspiring words for someone who is supposed to speak to a group, but I did sense this message: "Make the words matter."

The school was doing a good job of teaching different broadcasting techniques. Several of the teachers also worked in broadcasting, and they wisely stressed the need to pay dues in smaller markets. Sometimes that means working at a place for free while in school.

But there are a lot of people who work hard but still trash their careers.

That's what I decided to talk about—how we self-destruct.

I came up with these 10 suggestions:

1. Bad relationships can make you miserable at home and at work. When you marry someone, or even become seriously involved, you deal with more than just the person. You have to deal with the person's family history, and at some point, the family. If the family is a disaster, even the most mature adult coming out of that environment has wounds and scars. Be careful.

1 Corinthians 15:33: "Do not be misled: Bad company corrupts good character."

2. Most people know not to use drugs or drink heavily. But I've seen many people become involved with alcoholics and drug addicts and think, "I'll change them." Or think, "They love me, so they will change." In most cases, they don't change. In nearly every case, you can't be their close friend and/or spouse—and also their drug counselor. The most selfish people in the world are addicts. You can argue about it being a disease or a choice, but people who use drugs and drink heavily lie and really don't like anyone. Not you. Not themselves. They will drag you down emotionally, physically and financially.

Proverbs 23:21: "Drunkards and gluttons become poor."

3. Heavy use of credit cards and other significant debt is a killer. To make it in most professions means being patient, working for little money and living frugally. So many talented people start careers in media, teaching and other professions, and then pile up the bills. They quit and take a job that pays a few more bucks right now.

Proverbs 22:7: "The borrower is servant to the lender."

4. It's not how much you make; it's how much you keep.

Proverbs 13:7: "One man pretends to be rich, yet has nothing; another pretends to be poor, yet has great wealth."

5. Why should you be able to drive the same type of car or live in the same kind of home as your parents? They are decades older than you. When I was a young reporter in Savannah, my wife and I lived in a one-room slave's house next to the "big house." Never regretted it, and it makes for a good story when looking back on life. A dose of poverty and humility can be a good experience if we learn from it.

Proverbs 11:2: "When pride comes, then comes disgrace, but with humility comes wisdom."

6. Are you attracted to negative or positive people? Negative people don't care about you. They will drag you down, no matter their intent.

Proverbs 13:20: "He who walks with the wise grows wise, but a companion of fools suffers harm."

7. In the end, stay away from gossip and people who love to gossip. It's addicting and it can kill a career. If a person gossips about others, what does he say about you behind your back?

Proverbs 20:19: "A gossip betrays a confidence, so avoid a man who talks too much."

8. Not everyone has to hear your opinion of everything. Your boss doesn't care about your opinion of how the entire corporation or office should be run.

Proverbs 12:23: "A prudent man keeps his knowledge to himself, but the heart of fools blurts out folly."

9. Your boss is not your parent and not your friend. Your boss doesn't really care about your personal problems, even if it seems as if he or she does. The boss is there to get the job done. And part of being a boss is critiquing a person's work. Try to learn from correction and not take everything personally. Don't spend a lot of time saying, "I know I made a mistake, but I don't appreciate HOW I was told about it." Just admit you are wrong and fix it.

Proverbs 12:1: "Whoever loves discipline loves knowledge, but he who hates correction is stupid."

10. Don't give up when rejection comes. Don't give up when you make poor decisions (and you will). Don't surrender your in-

tegrity or believe the first person to say you are destined to fail (because someone will do that). For years, I carried a rejection letter from the *Richmond Times-Dispatch* in Virginia that said while my stories "showed enthusiasm," it would "be best to pursue another endeavor." Don't give up; get up again.

Proverbs 24:16: "Though a righteous man falls seven times, he rises again."

MAKING FRIENDSHIP MATTER

I have gone through significant changes in my life that have dramatically altered (diminished) my circle of friends. The best part about these seasons of our life is we come to realize the value of true friends and we also come to an even greater appreciation of our family. My experience has given me more compassion for those who have experienced a season of deep loneliness. Thanks for sharing your gift of words—and faith.

—Sandy Currier, Hudson

5

Friendship Has to be About Something

Nearly every vacation we take, my wife and I do something outdoors—usually hiking.

She's the type who'd love to sleep outside with the bugs and bears and every other critter in between. I like a place such as a Hampton or Residence Inn.

We compromise. We spend days hiking in the wilderness and nights in comfort.

Works well for both of us.

At this point you probably think I'm going to write about compromise being needed in any meaningful relationship.

OK, compromise is needed in any meaningful relationship.

But that's not my point.

Author C.S. Lewis wrote that friendship "must be about something."

Ever have a person either ask, "Can we be friends?" Or act as if she wanted to be your friend? And you asked yourself, "Why would I want to be her friend? Not only is she a bit strange, but we have absolutely nothing in common."

The key is the second part—having nothing in common.

As Lewis wrote in his book *The Four Loves*, "The very condition of having Friends is that we should want something else besides Friends. Where the truthful answer to the question 'Do you see the same truth?' would be 'I see nothing and I don't care about the truth; I only want a Friend.' No Friendship can arise—though affection of course may. There would be nothing for the Friendship to be about; and Friendship must be about something, even if it were only an enthusiasm for dominoes or white mice."

When Roberta and I take a vacation, we go to places such as Michigan's Upper Peninsula, the Blue Ridge Mountains of northern Virginia, Wyoming or Cedar Key, Fla. Those locations have two things in common: They are or are near small towns away from people and they are close to nature.

I learned to appreciate being away from people and being close to nature from my wife, who is from Greenville, Pa. The town is about 40 minutes east of Youngstown. It had a population of about 10,000 when Roberta was young; there are even fewer people today.

My wife grew up climbing trees, riding horses, and playing in the woods while wearing jeans, a sweatshirt and tennis shoes. She has never worn makeup or high heels. She can dress elegantly and look spectacular when the situation demands, but she'd rather leave her best clothes in the closet . . . forever!

I grew up in the Cleveland area going to ballgames and dreaming of working for a major newspaper, perhaps even in New York City. While in college a friend and I vacationed in New York several times. I loved the subway and the smog and spending time in the metropolis that may sulk, but never sleeps.

While Roberta liked to hear crickets creaking at night, I was more comfortable with sirens blaring.

Roberta and I started as friends. She liked sports. We'd play basketball or baseball (she hated softball; the ball was too big and she liked playing with boys). We'd play almost anything outside.

We also went to movies and to cheap restaurants. But it was obvious she loved being outside and active, and I did, too. We didn't do much hiking because I was not sure about this going-into-the-woods deal.

We dated for more than four years before we married in 1977.

We were friends first, and we were friends because we were more than attracted to each other's personalities and looks. Or at least, I was attracted to her looks. Obviously, sexual sizzle is part of it. But it can't be all or even most of it, as any couple will attest.

Or as Lewis wrote: "Those who cannot conceive of friendship as a substantive love but only as a disguise or elaboration of Eros betray the fact that they have never had a friend."

We had a friendship that was "about something." We liked being together, doing things together. More importantly, we knew that we didn't have to share every opinion, every interest and every activity. But we had to share some and we had to be open to learning new things from the other person.

Rather than "grow apart" as so many couples (and friends) do, we grew together. To do that, we had to be open to each other's interests and desires.

I'm writing this from a Residence Inn near Waynesboro, Va. If you have to look it up on the map, that's the point. It's away from most things and most people. I'm writing after we'd hiked seven miles in a place called the "Allegheny Highlands." It's near the Virginia-West Virginia border in Highland County, Virginia's least populated county with 3,000 residents.

It was one of those postcard days on the trail: sun sneaking through huge pine, popular and oak trees; stunning views of the 4,000-foot-high mountains in West Virginia; and no one else around.

We also walked through some old Confederate rifle and cannon pits at the start of the trail. A wild turkey sprinted about 100 yards in front of us.

Later we saw deer leap over fallen trees. Birds chirped, bees buzzed and the trail was mostly flat and mosquito-free. Whenever we have one of these wonderful hikes, I thank Roberta—because I wouldn't be doing this unless I had met her. I learned the outdoors from her, and it has become a major part of our relationship.

Obviously, our marriage and friendship is about more than hiking and vacations, but the more activities two people have in common, the more likely their relationship will survive.

In a book called *Soulcraft,* Douglas Webster writes, "Friendship is born of mutual respect, shared concern and common cause. It involves a meeting of the minds, an enjoyment of each other's company and the freedom to feel at home with one another."

Or as C.S. Lewis maintained: "It's about something . . ."

Not just someone.

That's why some people make close friends at work. The job not only is the starting point for the relationship, it also can be the foundation. Consider any house. You really don't *see* the foundation. The house is built on top of it. But the foundation holds it together, even as the house and yard go in different directions.

My best male friends are three guys who are part of a jail ministry team. They didn't start out as my closest friends. We began as guys with an interest in serving God and reaching inmates. We go into the Summit County Jail every Wednesday morning to run a 90-minute service for inmates. But we meet every Tuesday to plan the service and pray. In the process, we have learned a lot about each other and developed common bonds in other areas. But it began with jail ministry, and the demands of ministry ensure that we stay in close contact. We have done life together through the deaths of parents and the breakups of marriages, through new jobs and money problems.

But we also work together each week on the jail service.

Roberta is a gifted singer and has been a part of choirs for decades. That is a place where she has made some of her close friends. She is part of the jail ministry team, as is another friend, Gloria Williams.

Roberta would never have dreamed of singing in jail, if it weren't for me. Now she relishes being part of the ministry team.

Just as I would never have imagined that a way to relax was to walk (and sometimes sweat and grunt) more than five miles trudging over mountains, through thousands of trees and even hopping on rocks over a stream. Now I even go for shorter hikes alone, thanks to what I learned from Roberta.

C.S. Lewis also wrote: "It may be a common religion, common studies, a common profession, even a common recreation. All who share it will be our companions; but one or two or three who share something more will be our Friends."

I know of a pastor who had a hard time making close friends. He had a love of motorcycles. He joined a motorcycle group and made lots of friends. At first many of the bikers were suspicious of him; they figured he wanted to convert everyone and baptize them in the sink. Instead they learned he was passionate about bikes and he knew a lot about bikes. He didn't push his faith on the other bikers; he acted it out by being a good biker buddy. After a while some began to attend his church. A few became regular members.

But he didn't join the bikers to drag them to his church; he joined because he liked bikes.

He didn't worry that some people had lifestyles and opinions that differed from his. He made new and close friends as they talked more about mud flaps and mufflers.

All of us want friends.

All of us need friends.

But not all of us want to do what it takes to earn them.

How do we find friends?

Start with prayer. Ask God to show you if there is something that is preventing friendship. Then ask someone who knows reasonably well if there is part of your personality that may repel others. It's a scary question, but the answer may be life changing.

Search for some people who have *some* things—not *every* thing—in common with you.

Then go and do one of those things with them.

6

Saying No is OK

It started with a guy who wanted me to buy him a beer.

Not just a beer but a 40-ouncer. At 9:10 a.m. At a convenience store.

The guy recognized me from my jail ministry. Mr. 40-Ouncer was there with a friend. I could tell they needed some help. I offered to buy his buddy the Snapple in his hand. And I told him to get something to eat.

Mr. 40-Ouncer kept saying, "Come on, Terry, it's just a few bucks for a beer. Be a friend."

I said, "Get something to eat like your friend."

He said, "A man's gotta do what he's gotta do. Just give me the money and I'll buy the beer. Then you won't feel bad about buying it."

I said, "A man may gotta do what he has to do, but I still won't buy you the beer."

Mr. 40-Ouncer should have been a lawyer the way he loved to negotiate. Given the fact that he was in jail, he probably knows a few lawyers. Some guys who have spent a lot of time in jail know more than some lawyers—they've been studying the law and writing briefs.

While I alternated between feeling amused and annoyed with this stupid conversation about the merits of a 40-ouncer at

9 a.m., the man's buddy arrived with his hands full of pizza slices and said, "Just let him buy us the food already."

I bought them four slices of pizza and a couple of Snapples.

I never knew if Mr. 40-Ouncer got his beer.

I did know that I wasn't going to give either guy cash because it is a temptation . . . and there was plenty of food in the store. The men also were down the street from the Haven of Rest, Akron's city mission.

Did I know for certain the guy had a drinking problem? No.

But I do know an estimated 80 percent of the people in urban jails are addicted to something.

After reading this you may be wondering, "Just what is the point?"

During the conversation, I thought about buying the beer just to quiet the guy and make him happy. I don't like confrontation. But I was glad that I didn't bend.

It's much tougher to do when it's a family issue.

A friend issue.

Too often we think, "I want to be liked, so I will do this against my better judgment," and we do something against our better judgment that we know is wrong.

It's remarkable how many 30-year-olds turn into 13-year-olds when they move back home—at least in terms of wanting to be waited upon. They switch back to 30 when the bills arrive or when their parent says, "You don't bring that person under this roof all night. This is my house!"

"I'm not a kid anymore," they say.

And that can lead to a painful argument.

Ask any parent about the adult child who returns home because of money problems and doesn't pay much (or any) rent. But he has enough cash (or room on a credit card) to party a few times a week. He also expects his parent to do his washing and ironing, make breakfast and buy groceries.

Or the daughter who can't believe you painted her room—she

has been gone from home for about 10 years. And she is insulted when you ask her to help pay for the utilities and other expenses.

"I thought you loved me!" she whines through tears.

The real question is: Do we love our children enough to do what is right . . . and risk them not liking us?

A couple of pastors suggested that before we allow an adult child to move back in, we set guidelines such as:

- The child pays something for rent.
- He does his laundry, and perhaps some of yours, too.
- She does some chores.
- There is a time limit on how long the child will stay. Is he going back to school? Is she saving for a new place? How long will that take?
- No friends overnight. You have the right to veto any visitors. It's your house or apartment unless they are paying a huge share of the bills. Often people leaving jail want to come home for a while. That is understandable. But there are some friends from jail and the street that you must keep away.
- No drugs in the house. Have a policy on how to handle drinking.

There surely are other things that will come to mind—*write* them down and make both parties sign the paper.

You may get the "I thought you loved me" line fired back at you.

Say, "I love you enough to set guidelines to make this work for all of us."

Helping is only helpful and godly when it's constructive.

I know some people who have problems handling money. They say they need to pay the electric bill. I ask to see the bill. Then I write a check to the utility company. They may view it as a lack of trust, but it's a good way to ensure the electric company doesn't shut off the power.

This is not about helping someone in a crisis with health issues, etc. It is about having the strength to say "no" when it's easier to say "yes." It's about not allowing people to drop their guilt on us—because we have been making better choices.

It's realizing, "We rarely change until our pain exceeds the fear of change."

Those words are from Pastor Rick Warren (author of *The Purpose Driven Life*). Sometimes we hurt the process of change that God and life in general are pushing on the troubled person by taking away that person's pain.

It's hard to know when trying to help eventually hurts, when patience ceases to be a virtue and instead fuels a vice.

Prayer helps. So does realizing that doing the right thing often is the hard thing.

A lot tougher than not buying a beer first thing in the morning.

- 7 -

Faith, Race and the Red Barn

Red Barn restaurants have gone the way of "See Rock City" signs on real barns.

Red Barn was a second-rate hamburger joint; it served very thin, greasy patties on a stale bun. You may have wanted the burger your way, but you got it the way they felt like making it that day.

At least that's how I remember the Red Barn on Buckeye Road, not far from Benedictine High in Cleveland.

Red Barn became an after-school haven for students at Benedictine in the early 1970s. It was a place for dry french fries and sad shakes. It was a place to talk about teachers and coaches and music and, yes, girls.

Girls were a mystery at our all-boys school. Now I'm glad the school was all-boys because it took all the agony and drama of dating out of the building. The way some teenage girls dress today, I have no clue how boys make it through the day and remember anything their teachers have said.

Girls or no girls, my guess is today's high school kids have places like Red Barn—McDonald's, coffee shops, the mall.

And in 40 years, some of these kids will look back—as I recently did while driving down Buckeye Road—and try to figure out where exactly the hangout stood.

Red Barn is long gone. So are many of my memories of the place, but not all of them.

While I don't recall many specific conversations at the Red Barn, I do remember this: I felt safe there.

It was the early 1970s, and the east side neighborhood no longer was home to Slovaks and other Eastern Europeans. Most had moved to Parma or Garfield Heights or another suburb. The neighborhood was "changing," and not just in terms of race. It was changing economically, as the middle class left for Shaker Heights, Cleveland Heights and Euclid.

At Red Barn, we didn't think much about it. Benedictine was at least 35 percent black, and not because of court order. Parents sent their boys to the school for a solid education, even if they weren't Catholic.

Galatians 3:28 reads: "There is neither Jew nor Greek [Gentile], slave nor free, male nor female, for you are all one in Christ Jesus."

While there were no females, and I'm not sure if there were any Jews in the school, there were kids from several denominations. Some black, some white. Some wealthy, some middle class, some poor.

Those distinctions didn't matter on our sports teams. The question was: Could you play?

And at Red Barn, there seemed to be little class, religious or racial distinctions. That was rather remarkable in a city that has been divided and torn apart by racial strife.

Yes, some areas of the cafeteria seemed more white than black ... or more black than white.

Part of the reason was racial, but some of it was kids wanting to hang around with others from their old neighborhood or with those who played the same sport. Obviously, not everyone was thrilled with all members of a different race. But we didn't have racial fights, even if we had some issues with how others talked and acted.

When I was on the junior varsity basketball team, I was one of the few whites in uniform. The baseball team, however, had only a few blacks. Most of those athletes preferred to run track in the spring.

For the athletes in these sports, there were some major life lessons to be learned: Sometimes you are the majority, sometimes you aren't. Sports and friendships are bigger and more important than race . . . just as a true heartfelt faith means more than denominational identity.

I came from a religious mix of a home. My mother was Protestant, at least in name. She rarely went to church. When she did, it was with my father to the Catholic church. I also went to church with my dad.

But when I stayed with my grandparents, I attended a Presbyterian church several times a year. What I learned from that experience was to avoid spitball fights between denominations, and what was most important was to find the right church, regardless of the denominational name.

One of the fastest ways to put aside denominational differences is to have people from different churches serve in a soup kitchen, or repair a house or take food to the elderly.

Watch how the mission is what matters most.

Watch how they will join hands in prayer.

Watch how they will encourage each other without worrying about how a certain group views issues such as evolution, the Second Coming of Christ, or when and how people should be baptized.

What does this have to do with Red Barn and an inner-city Catholic school?

My friends at Red Barn were both black and white.

Some had Catholic backgrounds, some did not.

Some were athletes, some were not.

Most of us were good students and we stayed out of serious trouble.

At the time, I didn't know 1 Corinthians 15:33: "Bad company corrupts good character."

I did have a friend whose mother warned him, "You keep hangin' out with them street boys, you gonna end up in jail with them."

He stopped and joined our group.

The Benedictine monks took Catholicism seriously. But even more serious was their commitment to Christ, their vows of communal living and poverty, and their insistence that a good Catholic (and Christian) must give to and serve the poor.

While all the monks were white, they wouldn't tolerate racial slurs during the early 1970s. Benedictine continues to stay strong in one of Cleveland's difficult neighborhoods. The monks and lay teachers talk about "a calling" to serve young men in the city, especially in a time when many of these young men don't have a father in the home.

Before attending Benedictine, I had limited contact with people of other races. My grandparents (the Protestants) lived in a mostly minority neighborhood, and at times I was the only white kid playing baseball with the kids on that block. But I was so young and so into sports, I didn't notice the fact that I was the minority—nor did it seem like a big deal to the other kids in the pickup games. But that stopped by the time I was about 10 as I spent less time at my grandparents' home.

It was at Benedictine where I had to face racial attitudes that came from growing up in a white suburb. It's where I learned to love Motown, and it's also where I made friends and had dinner at homes where I was the only white at the table.

And then there was Red Barn, which was truly integrated when school let out.

Red Barn is gone. Benedictine is not as large as it was in the 1970s.

But the lessons from those places stick with me.

Harry's Law Of Life

Harry Watson was a man who listened far more than he talked, a man who trusted far more than he judged.

When his daughter, Renee, went out of town to take her law exams, he stayed at the hotel with her. That way she knew he was there for her—praying. And if she wanted to talk, he'd listen. If not, she could rest, and he'd sit near her, quietly.

Early in her college career, Renee wanted to quit law school. Harry insisted that she press on and become a lawyer. She had the right stuff; he was sure of it.

Harry was once a star salesman at Procter & Gamble, yet he seemed to lack what you'd expect from most salesmen. He spoke softly, dressed conservatively, refused to make grand promises and perhaps even looked a bit embarrassed when asking you to buy his product.

None of that was a pose; it was pure Harry. And his customers knew it. They trusted him. Harry said he had little to do with his success. He gave credit to God and to Proctor & Gamble for having excellent products to sell.

But Harry also was a man who found himself broken after a divorce, which put him on a tear-soaked road to faith. It led him to slowly back away from a lucrative corporate job to become involved in prison ministry. At 59, Harry was living off stock options, savings and donations, as he became the volunteer chaplain at the Summit County Jail.

Harry and his second wife, Sandra, lived modestly for 17 years. Sandra may have set a record for cutting coupons in their town of Munroe Falls. There were times when they sweated a bit as the bills came, but it always seemed a check or cash showed up just in time.

The Rev. Ronald Fowler, former pastor of the Arlington Church of God in Akron, once said, "God always shows up, but he's rarely early."

The Watsons can attest to that.

When Harry began visiting prisoners about 30 years ago, the deputies were not thrilled. They made him stay in the lobby for more than an hour, hoping he would become discouraged and go home. But Harry would sit there, read his Bible and wait.

He never complained; he always was polite.

For 20 years, he was given free run of the jail. Even the deputies who had no interest in God and thought ministry behind bars was a waste of time had tremendous respect for Harry Watson.

Harry attended a conservative Baptist church where the music was southern gospel, but his prison ministry group included people from four different churches. Two were from minority churches, and one was charismatic. The music at the services was rockin', hand-clappin', feet-stompin' urban gospel. Harry believed the biblical gospel message was the cake and not open to debate, but the cake could be frosted in various ways.

He hated denominational spitball fights or lofty theological debates. There were too many beaten-down men in jail who needed a simple message of faith to worry about such matters.

In 2010, Harry died at the age of 76. He was in jail three weeks before heading to surgery, from which he never recovered.

But this story isn't just about Harry Watson. It is a reminder that there are many silent saints among us. They work in rest homes and hospitals and schools and with youth teams and music groups. They hate being the center of attention.

"Preach the gospel always, use words if necessary," is their motto, based on a quote that some attribute to St. Francis of Assisi.

At Harry's funeral, former inmates showed up. So did highly placed law enforcement officials. As did people from Akron's Haven of Rest Ministry and some old friends from the corporate world.

As his wife said, "Harry would be embarrassed by all this attention."

You may know a Harry Watson; go ahead, embarrass that person with a little praise. It will be good for your soul.

I dedicated my first *Faith and You* book: "To Harry Watson, I want to be like you when I grow up."

At the age of 57, that still holds true for me.

WHEN GOD SHOWS UP IN UNUSUAL PLACES

I sometimes feel you are writing to me alone out here in the world. Thanks for being such a great writer and influence in my life.

—Bob Slaga, Brunswick

- 9 -

When God Says You're Not in Control

I could easily write about how watching a fiery orange ball of a sunset over Lake Superior attests to the power of God. That is true.

It also is very warm and fuzzy, and worthy of a picture post-card.

But spending nearly two weeks in Michigan's Upper Peninsula speaks to me of God's power in a different way.

My wife and I have made at least six trips to the U.P. in the last seven years. We love this place. The shoreline is spectacular, the hiking challenging, the wilderness aptly named. The first time we came here was in late June. That's when we encountered the bugs.

They really aren't bugs; they are like Blackhawk helicopters that swirl around your head. Those are just the mosquitoes. Then come the stable flies and the black flies. They travel in packs of millions and can suck the blood out of a bear in about 15 seconds.

Then there are ticks.

OK, most of the bugs are not that bad. Only a few will actually kill you. The rest just make you wish you were dead.

By August the worst of them are gone, but the bears still prowl. Most years there is a story that begins with someone who just pulled a blueberry pie out of the oven. It's always blueberry because they love blueberries up here. They have blueberry festivals. Bears also worship blueberries. So, the story goes, the bear smells the blueberry pie, smashes the kitchen window and eats its prize.

Unless you happen to have a bazooka around the house, not much can stop a bear from coming through a window after a pie.

But not even a bazooka can stall the big black flies or the little sneaky "no-see-ums." You can't see them, but you can hear them buzz until you want to stick your head in a bear's mouth and just end it.

The good thing is the snow eventually comes and wipes out the bugs. It also causes the bears to sleep for months.

The bad thing is, the snow comes.

The eastern part of the U.P. receives about 200 inches of snow a year. That's a mere dusting, say those in the western part. They insist 300 inches of snow is a good winter. They put little flags on top of their mailboxes and car antennas so they can be spotted when buried in a snowdrift that seems to be taller than the Terminal Tower.

What Yoopers (that's what they call themselves) have learned is that so much of life can't be controlled. During one of their two-feet-in-12-hours blizzards—with whiteouts—people just don't drive. They barely step outside. They just wait until it's over.

I don't like to wait for anything—but especially not for the weather to change.

Many Yoopers live near Lake Superior, which is about the size of South Carolina. Its average depth is 482 feet. Its average temperature is about 40 degrees. It has caused more than 350 shipwrecks. People drown every year in its vicious riptides. It also is the world's largest freshwater lake by surface area. It's so clear that you can watch the muskies swim up and bite your toes off. (I've never seen that happen; I've just heard stories about it.)

This summer, a moose wandered into a park in downtown Marquette and refused to leave for more than week. They just don't listen, those moose.

The Yoopers love to tell these stories about bears and bugs and moose and foot-eating fish just to watch the faces of the "trolls."

We are the trolls. A troll is anyone who lives below the Mackinac Bridge.

Beyond the beauty, bears and bugs are the people.

One Sunday I went to a small nondenominational church in a town on Lake Superior where the biggest employer was shutting down. This is a place where people do indeed pinch their pennies, eat pasties and catch walleye and lake trout while trying to figure out what to do when there is too much month and not enough money. About 25 people were in the pews, and everyone knew everyone else's names—even if you just showed up, as my wife and I did. People introduced themselves as naturally as they would take their next breath.

As the service neared the end, a woman stood and talked about trying to buy a car. She didn't have enough money. It became rather complicated, covering two dealerships, a used Dodge Dakota, a used Chevy and a better deal on Dodge Neon. She told of breaking into tears at the dealership, then heading to the ladies' room for prayer. When she came back, she cut a deal on a 1999 Neon.

The car had some problems, but she added, "It came with four pretty good tires."

People in the pews applauded.

An older man stood and mentioned that today was his 40th wedding anniversary. He was a minister from another small church in town, had moved to Green Bay, but something happened with a job, and he was back in this small town. He had a lead on "a pretty good job," and people applauded, then prayed for him to get the job.

Finally, a middle-aged man with huge, heavily tattooed arms rolled to the front of the church in his wheelchair. He had the face and torso of a man who looked strong enough to punch a hole in the side of an iron freighter on the lake. His legs ended about a foot below his waist.

He cleared his throat. He took off his red baseball cap and nervously began to twist it. His voice cracked as he said, "I didn't always live how God wanted."

He paused and twisted the cap again.

He explained, "When they took off my first leg, they didn't know if I'd make it."

He made it.

But then they had to take off the second leg.

He said he had vision, a white light before that surgery. He said he sang a few hymns as they rolled him into the operating room. When he awoke, his other leg was gone, but his family was there.

"We prayed to God, thanking him," he said. "God is good."

He told his story quietly, humbly. He kept twisting the cap. As he rolled his wheelchair to the back of the church, people applauded. He looked embarrassed, but he wanted people to know that God was there for him even when his legs were gone.

The Upper Peninsula is a land of 16,412 square miles, millions of trees and fewer than 300,000 people. It's rugged beauty, wild weather and gritty people.

It's also a place where God reminds us who is in charge—and it's sure not us.

Flowers Bloom Where
Blood Ran

The Virginia town of McDowell probably looks much as it did on May 8, 1862.

There are a couple of old stores, and you get the feeling that if you blink while driving through, you'll miss the town completely.

It's in Highland County, population 2,321. Not far from the West Virginia border, it proudly claims to be the state's least-populated county.

It's on U.S. 250, a stomach-twisting road that winds through the mountains. The nearest McDonald's is 25 miles and about 150 years away.

The county initially balked at joining the Confederacy, then changed its mind after the first Civil War battle at Fort Sumter. In May of 1862, about 12,500 men battled in McDowell, a town that today has a population of 442.

From the top of Sitlington's Hill, where much of the battle took place, you can sense God's presence. It's in the trees, the mountains, the clouds so close that you swear they will drop down and embrace you. Ten men from McDowell fought for the Union, many more with the Confederates. It's where friends and family yelled greetings to each other from opposite sides of the battle line before the shooting began.

This is not a place where the Civil War is remembered with Stonewall Jackson ice cream or hamburgers at Honest Abe's Bar and Grill. Just a couple of road signs mention troop positions.

You can follow a winding path up Sitlington's Hill to retrace how the Confederates established their position.

Or you can hike through shrubs, weeds, rocks, ditches and a deep gorge, as my wife and I did when we missed the original trailhead. Turned out we were on part of the same trail over which Confederate General Stonewall Jackson led his men. On this day, we were the only ones there. It's that way most days. This is not a park with a tour guide. There are no statues of generals along the way, no old cannons on top.

But there are a few picnic tables at the crest, where you can see 50 miles into West Virginia on a clear day. It's a place to listen to birds and hear chipmunks scurry through the woods.

It's hard to imagine anything horrible happening here.

But it's where men died and were wounded on the steep mountain. Stretchers were made of blankets and empty muskets to carry the injured down to the Presbyterian church, still standing.

It's where a small field turned red with blood, and where there are holes in the ground that once upon a time were rifle pits.

It's where Jackson, on horseback, sucked on lemons during the battle. He would raise his right arm in the air because he felt a little out of balance, believing one of his legs was shorter than the other. And he believed that if he swallowed pepper, his left leg would ache.

Jackson was instrumental in creating Sunday school classes for blacks at a large Presbyterian church in Lexington, Va. That was before the war when it was illegal in Virginia to teach blacks to read—which he did, so they could learn the Bible.

Jackson was an artillery instructor from nearby Virginia Military Academy, and today he still is respected in the black community of Lexington.

Yet he fought for the South.

Historians say McDowell was the first victory in Jackson's "Shenandoah Campaign," still studied in military colleges. He drove the Union forces back to what is now West Virginia. McDowell is a footnote in the war. Famed Civil War historian Shelby Foote said it barely deserved to be called a battle.

But more than 150 were killed, another 670 wounded.

In the book *Stonewall in the Valley,* Robert Tanner wrote, "Compared to later engagements of the war, the fight at McDowell was an affair of gnats."

Think about it: 150 dead . . . 670 wounded . . . an affair of gnats?

More than 620,000 died in the Civil War. More than 20,000 were killed or wounded in a single day at the battle of Antietam— just months after McDowell.

I hear people today say that they've never seen our country more angry, more divided, but a sense of history helps. McDowell is a place where you can feel it during a time when God looked down at America and wept.

Wyoming, Moose & God

I don't think much about heaven, other than I want to go there. Some images of heaven depict angels floating on clouds and playing harps, or a never-ending church service where people sing and pray until they drop.

I doubt either portrait is correct. But there are times when I've had a taste of heaven. It's often happened when I've been out West.

My wife and I hike in the Black Hills, especially Custer and Wind Cave parks in South Dakota. More than 3,000 bison roam free, and odds are if you walk for even an hour, you'll find a few of them. Most of the time they are standing and eating grass . . . or sleeping in the grass.

They act a lot like classy cows.

But each year they kill a few tourists who walk up and shove a camera in their faces. When you hear that bison are on the trail, you either take a different trail or you make a wide circle around them.

One late fall evening my wife and I were hiking the Black Hills under a scarlet sunset. The long grass—some of it is called buffalo grass—was golden and swaying in the wind. Earlier in the hike we had seen a herd of at least a dozen antelope. It seemed that no one else was hiking that day; it was as if we had the park to ourselves.

We walked down a hill on a narrow trail that soon would lead up another hill. As we reached the ridge in between, the ground began to shake. We heard a roar behind us.

We turned . . . and saw at least 100 bison, racing along our trail!

We had seen bison many times on our previous trips, but never this . . . never a massive single-file stampede.

They were sprinting at us, and bison can run fast—they've been clocked at 30 mph.

We jumped off the ridge trail and rolled about 20 feet down a small hill. Keeping low, lying on our stomachs, we watched them run by.

The ground shook. Their hooves pounded. They snorted.

In less than a minute, it was over.

Silence.

Down one hill they went, up the next . . . and they were gone.

A few moments later we walked up the hill and looked for them.

Gone.

Not even one.

It was as if we had dreamed the entire scene.

I have a feeling heaven is far more like this than people sitting around, strumming on harps and singing "Kumbaya."

I have a feeling that heaven is wild. It's unexpected. It's God's power and God's creatures unleashed in unimaginable ways.

I had another experience like the barreling buffalo . . . only not with bison and not in South Dakota.

I was in Wyoming. It was the day before the Browns were to play in Denver. Rather than spend the day in the city, I drove three hours north, across the Colorado line into southern Wyoming. I drove down roads where I saw more pronghorn antelope than I did cars or people.

I drove down roads where one sign read: "Next services, 34 hours."

I drove down roads where, when it snows, crews drop gates and close the interstates until the storm passes.

I drove down roads under high skies and huge clouds that seemed to rise to the heavens.

I drove down roads through miles of open pasture with horses acting as if they owned the land.

I drove down roads that made me think of a line from novelist Dan O'Brien: "You have a sense that everyone can see you, but no one is looking." That may bother people who are uneasy about all the rugged, lonely hills and valleys.

For those who love a crowd and the 50-percent-off sale at the mall, a state with 522,830 people and an estimated 550,000 antelope may not have much appeal.

I've been to Wyoming at least a dozen times. On each visit I think how humans have not tamed the land. Some mountains are too high, some rivers too wild, some storms too fierce. I know there are days when Wyoming can seem like hell on earth . . . during a blizzard, or a dust storm, or when you have a blown radiator in the middle of nowhere and no one around to call for help because there is no cell phone service.

But I didn't think of that as I drove south of Laramie. I saw several herds of pronghorns—0 here, 25 there, at least 50 on top of the hill ahead. For 10 miles, not a single car was on the road.

In Isaiah 65:17, God says, "Behold, I will create new heavens and a new earth." I had a taste of it as I drove west on Wyoming 130 into the Snowy Mountains. They rose 10,000 feet with the sun peeking behind snow-capped peaks.

Rather than spend time wondering how such a place was created, I was in awe of God's hand and power behind it all.

Then I saw a truck on the other side of the road, with a man standing near it, staring into the woods. I slowed and spotted a huge horse with antlers . . . only it was a moose in a clearing. I stopped and walked over to the man.

"There's four of 'em," he said.

A female moose and two young ones ambled out from bushes, joining the bull. We silently watched them for about five minutes, me wondering what exactly got into God when he created a strange creature like a moose. Sheer entertainment, I suppose.

Finally, the four moose disappeared into the woods. The man and I left, nodding to each other but not saying a word.

First Corinthians 2:9 reads: "As it is written: 'No eye has seen, no ear has heard, no mind has conceived what God has prepared for those who love him.'"

But on certain days in the West, I've been given a glimpse.

12

Moving On When Your Heart Feels Like Quitting

In 2008, Father Dominic Mondzelewski nearly fell as he got out of bed. Just taking a step burned his lungs, his heart pounded as if it were about to burst. He couldn't take five steps without having to sit.

The Benedictine monk prayed: "Lord, if you want me, I'm ready. I don't know how much more of this I can handle."

Now Dominic is 69. He has been at Regina Health Center in Richfield since 2007, suffering from congestive heart failure. He also has battled staph and other infections in his knee. There was a case of cellulitis and other health issues.

When one problem seemed solved, two more showed up.

For 41 years, Dominic was a social studies teacher at Benedictine High School. He was principal from 1977–94, the longest anyone has held that job. During parts of his career, he coached tennis, junior varsity baseball and cross-country.

"I used to throw batting practice to my players," he said. "I played half-court pickup basketball well into my 40s."

Juggling three jobs was the norm. He said Mass at St. Lawrence parish on weekends, in between his school duties.

Dominic was one of my favorite teachers at Benedictine. I graduated in 1973, but 10 years later I was at the school playing basketball with him, some other monks and friends. He was a star baseball player at Benedictine, a natural athlete whose movements were fluid.

Now his days are spent building up the strength to walk 50 yards down the hall to therapy. He talks on the phone with friends. He reads and watches sports on television.

"My life is totally different," he said. "I never expected this."

How many of us have said the same thing?

It could be anything from suddenly becoming disabled to dealing with a severely ill parent or child. It could be losing a career, a house or a life that you thought would just roll along unchanged.

"If you asked me five years ago if I could handle this right now, I don't know what I'd have said," Dominic said. "After I prayed that day for the Lord to take me, I thought of the letter from St. Paul where he prayed the same thing—but God wanted Paul here."

Dominic meant Philippians 1:22-24: "If I am to go on living in the body, this will mean fruitful labor for me. . . . I desire to depart and be with Christ, which is better by far; but it is more necessary for you that I remain in the body."

Dominic said he hasn't spent much time asking God the "Why?" question. Having officiated over so many funerals and wakes, he knows there is no good answer to why certain things happen. They just do.

Dominic thought of when Job confronted God about all his trials, and God didn't answer the question.

Instead, in Job 38:4, God says: "Where were you when I laid the earth's foundation?"

Dominic sometimes thinks back to Feb. 27, 2006. He was relatively healthy, teaching at Benedictine and serving as the pastor at St. Lawrence. He hurt his knee when he tripped over a chair. That led to the surgeries, the infections—and then his heart began to fail.

There were nights when he stared at the ceiling wondering, "How did this happen to me?"

But he is determined not to dwell on that.

"I miss going to the football and basketball games at Benedictine," he said. "I miss teaching. I miss a lot of my old life. But God has taught me patience. I look every day at the death notices in the paper, and I see so many who have died who are younger than me. I remind myself that I have had a blessed life."

Dominic is doing ministry from his room at Regina. Friends call for prayer and advice. Some residents stop in for blessings and company. He remembers how his schedule was so packed before. Now he has time to talk and listen to people.

"I don't know when, or if, I'll be able to leave here," he said. "I have made progress, but it is slow. But I find God still has things for me to do. It's not what I used to do, but I'm not bitter, I'm not frustrated. I ask God each day to give me patience."

He paused.

"There are still a lot of blessings in life. I just have to keep the right attitude and I find them."

DEALING WITH JERKS— AND THAT INCLUDES ME

I needed the reminder that I cannot change others, but I can change my attitude. Patience with others and with me is hard sometimes, but prayer is so powerful. I shared your column with two friends. I read it aloud to my friend Michelle and we talked about it. I also called my friend Betty to make sure she didn't miss it. She called later to thank me.

—Karen Corrigan, Lakewood

13

My Inner Jerk

He lives in me, and I'm not talking about the spirit of God.

I mean the Inner Jerk.

Not long ago I was on the Stairmaster at a health club. A guy named Rick came up to me. We're not close friends, but we work out at the same place and get along great.

He mentioned an event that I was supposed to attend, but we disagreed about when it was. Instead of accepting that there was a mix-up about the dates, I lashed out at the poor guy.

I told him he was wrong.

Then I told him why he was wrong.

I asked—OK, I sort of sneered as I nearly shouted—why he would know my schedule better than I know my schedule.

I insisted that I was right, and I demanded to know why we were even talking about this.

He stared at me as if I had dropped in from another planet and was demon possessed.

All along I kept hearing this quiet voice—I call it the whisper of the Holy Spirit—saying, "Just shut up already."

One of my favorite verses is from Proverbs 10:19: "When words are many, sin is not absent, but he who holds his tongue is wise."

But my tongue kept wagging. I should have been flagged for verbal piling-on.

"What is with you?" Rick asked. "I've never seen you like this!"

As he said that I remembered the advice found in the New Testament book of James: "[T]he tongue is a small part of the body, but it makes great boasts. Consider what a great forest is set on fire by a small spark. The tongue also is a fire. . . . It corrupts the whole person, sets the whole course of his life on fire. . . ." (James 3:5-6)

I hate to think of how many relationships I have burned with my tongue.

In the third chapter of James, we read: "All kinds of animals, birds, reptiles and creatures of the sea are being tamed and have been tamed by man, but no man can tame the tongue. . . . With the tongue we praise our Lord and Father, and with it we curse men, who have been made in God's likeness." (James 7-9)

After I attacked the guy at the health club with a verbal jackhammer, I began telling him my troubles. Remarkably, he was patient with me, even wondering out loud if he had said anything to ignite the outburst.

The only thing he had done was to interrupt the mental pity party at which I was the honored guest.

About 20 minutes after my eruption, I apologized to him.

He said, "Wow, I had no idea you could be like that."

I started to say, "Neither did I," but then I stopped.

Instead I said, "It's in there. I hate it when it comes out."

The Inner Jerk lurks in all of us.

This is not about the times an edge in a personality and a sharp tone is needed. I've been the durable power of healthcare for several elderly people who didn't have much money and were intimidated when dealing with hospitals and doctors. A few times I've had to push harder to make sure they received the needed medical attention.

I have never regretted that, because the situation was important, and I was standing up for someone who couldn't do it for herself.

But this event in the health club was not like that. It was all about me.

I wanted to vent. I had the *right* to vent, because I was having a long and difficult day. It was as if I were looking for an excuse to cut loose on someone. It was selfish, assuming that my feelings mattered more than those of someone else.

We live in a society that encourages venting, yelling, name-calling and harsh put-downs. They fuel many talk shows. Some newspaper and Internet columnists make a living by jacking up the heat and the venom as they unleash their opinions. In some places it's encouraged.

While there is a certain twisted entertainment value to the behavior, it can be incredibly destructive on a personal level.

That day at the health club, Rick forgave me.

We talked about our lives. We both had had people close to us in intensive care at a local hospital. Rick's situation had recently ended and was even more discouraging than the one I faced.

Later I thought of a story that Ron Grinker, the famed NBA agent, told me before his death. A devout Jew, he had heard a sermon about 12 people in a room. Each was asked to pack all of his or her problems in a bag and put the bags in the middle of the room.

"Then each person was allowed to open all the bags and pick one to carry," Grinker said. "Nearly everyone was surprised at how much trouble each person had. Nearly everyone picked their own bag of problems because they didn't seem so bad after all."

That's something to remember the next time the Inner Jerk wants to be heard.

- 14 -

Why Am I Always Annoyed?

Supposedly, God allows us to deal with difficult people so we can learn something.

Here's one lesson: "I don't *like* annoying people."

Not sure that's the real spiritual bottom line.

Annoying people are supposed to teach us patience.

They are supposed to stretch our ability to love and help those who don't give us much in return.

They are supposed to help us grow and mature, even if they refuse to do the same.

I understand all of that.

Dealing with the elderly can be demanding, depending upon the person. Many of them are battling depression because they have lost so much—a spouse, a job, health, mobility, status.

One of the hardest days for some of us is when we must tell an older person, "I don't think you should drive anymore."

Often that person gives us a look that screams: "Who are *you* to tell *me* that? I was driving long before you were born!"

Older people may not say a word, but tears run down their cheeks. They know you are right. But they hate it. They hate growing old. They hate being dependent on someone else. They hate what has happened to their life.

They may even hate it when they lash out at the people trying to help them.

But it happens.

Some of the best of us will turn into difficult people as time takes away our vision and reaction time behind the wheel.

I have several friends who can't drive for reasons ranging from economic to health.

From them, I've learned that it's no fun to ride the bus because it usually means taking at least two buses to cover what would be a 15-minute car ride.

I've learned that some people who ride the bus have emotional problems, and they can engage in some scary and strange conversations.

And that angry teenagers swear and strut up and down the aisle, daring other riders to tell them to sit down and shut up.

And that you can't control who sits next to you. And, yes, hygiene can be an issue.

Most people on the bus are not like this. They are reasonable and polite, just wanting to get to their job, to the store, and then home.

But a few difficult people can terrorize the bus, and they seem to know how far they can push it without the driver deciding to call the police.

What I've learned from my friends' stories about the bus is that I'm grateful I have a car. And that if you know someone who doesn't drive, offer that person a ride. Many are too ashamed to ask.

Their frustration about not having a car can cause them to become angry over other things in their life.

And with other people.

*   *   *

All of us are selfish, to some extent. That means we are probably a difficult person to someone else. Maybe you have an easy time admitting this, but I don't. A friend once said, "If only everyone would just look at things like this, everything would be OK."

She meant seeing the world through her eyes and with her point of view.

Not long after she said it, we both laughed. She knew it sounded arrogant. I knew that I have often thought the same thing, even if I never said it out loud.

Bet there have been days when most of us have thought: "If everyone would just take my advice, the world would be a better place."

Would it?

Really?

I never thought deeply about that. Maybe the world would be a better place for me, but I'm not even sure of that. Because when I start playing The Grand Designer, I create a mental universe that is free of pain and stress—for me.

Am I selfish?

Years ago I would have denied it. I would have insisted that I care about other people, that I do some good things. But as I began to read the Bible and all the passages about sin, I realized that selfishness is at the heart of sin. When I lie, it's usually about trying to make my life easier, to save me some grief. When I gossip, it's to make me sound smart—raising myself up while putting someone else down.

An eternal question is, "Are people naturally good or naturally selfish?"

Someone once told me that we are born selfish. Just look at a little kid. No one has to teach a child to scream, "Mine!"

Most parents don't need to tell children, "Quit sharing your toys and being so nice! You need to be a spoiled brat!"

The truth is that some of us fight that 2-year-old inside of us for the rest of our lives.

Don't think selfishness is a problem?

Answer this: Are most of your thoughts about you or someone else?

I know that when something happens, my first thought often is: "How will this affect my life?"

In too many conversations, I am not listening intently. I'm waiting for the other guy to shut up so I can talk.

Recently I was in the middle of writing. A friend called with a report about someone who is terminally ill. My friend had been taking care of this person, and it was emotionally draining. I was listening to what he said, but part of me was thinking, "I hope we can cut this short so I can go back and finish writing."

And the subject of that column was selfishness!

The reason I bring this up is not guilt. It's not about how we all need to sell everything we own and give it to the poor. Or quit our jobs and move to India to work with the social outcasts. It's not about putting ourselves in a position to suffer just for the sake of being in pain.

Most of all, it's not about letting certain people who are social sponges suck the life out of us and the dollars from our bank account. It's not selfish to rest when tired. Or to take a vacation. Or to exercise or to eat healthy food.

But it's not natural for me to be a giving, loving, patient, understanding person—all the things that the Apostle Paul writes about in 1 Corinthians Chapter 13.

When I look in the mirror or my soul, I do understand when the Old Testament prophet Jeremiah writes in 17:9: "The heart is deceitful above all things and beyond cure. Who can understand it?"

He is not saying we're hopelessly miserable. To me, it means that my battle with myself is spiritual.

As Jeremiah writes in the same chapter (17:14): "Heal me, O Lord, and I will be healed. Save me, and I will be saved."

So often, when I do the right thing and help someone the right way, I get tremendous satisfaction. But it is a major spiritual battle to get started. Faith begins with obedience, not feelings.

There is nothing wrong with sometimes asking, "What about me?"

But I do need to pray that I don't try to make everything about me.

*　　*　　*

When I admit to being a selfish person, it becomes easier to deal with difficult people.

In Matthew 13:24-30, Jesus tells the parable of The Weeds. It's about why God gives us time to grow—and why there are difficult and bad people in the world.

One of the themes is this: When someone annoys us, do we remember when we had problems? And that we still have some problems?

In Matthew 13:24-26, Jesus said: "The kingdom of heaven is like a man who sowed good seed in his field. But while everyone was sleeping, his enemy came and sowed weeds among the wheat, and went away. When the wheat sprouted and formed heads, then the weeds also appeared."

It's a fact that no matter where we are, bad situations and difficult people will appear.

In verses 27-29, Jesus added: "The owner's servants came to him and said, 'Sir, didn't you sow good seed in your field? Where then did the weeds come from?'"

"An enemy did this," he replied.

The servants asked him, "Do you want us to go and pull them up?"

"No," he answered, "because while you are pulling the weeds, you may root up the wheat with them. Let both grow together until the harvest."

Jesus doesn't want any of us to be choked by the weeds, but he knows many of us come from bad family situations. We need time to learn to grow out of the family mess.

Jesus also expects us to be patient with ourselves, and with each other. He seems to be asking us to remember the time when we were far from God and people were patient and kind with us.

What if God had said, "He's a weed; pull him up. Get him out of here."

Where would some of us be?

The weeds can be anger ... self-pity ... pride ... age ... physical or emotional problems.

Some of us need to take medication to stay out of the weeds, but we won't do it.

Some of us need to go to meetings to stay straight and sober because drugs or alcohol are choking us . . . but pride keeps us from admitting we need help.

Some of us need forgiveness, but we are afraid to sincerely talk to God about that.

Some of us need to deal with our own issues rather than dwell on the problems of others. And being patient with others does make us better, along with helping them.

A word of caution: This is not meant to allow abusive people to trample us. It's not about bringing addicted people back into our lives after they have broken our trust several times. It's not about permitting someone to humiliate and verbally attack us.

But it is saying that we can deal with those who are cranky and those who seem a bit stuck on themselves and their problems. It means that we can find a way to listen more than we talk. It means that we can begin to learn to see the world through another person's eyes, rather than wonder why that person doesn't see it our way.

Yes, God can use difficult people to help us grow ... especially when we remember that we can be difficult, too.

15

What Are You Carrying Around?

Ever spend days mentally replaying a conversation?

Or nights staring at the ceiling, thinking about something said to you, and then coming up with all the clever and sarcastic things you wanted to say but couldn't think of at the time?

Are you easily offended?

Most of us don't think so, but if we go over and over conversations or times when we believed we were insulted, then we probably are too easily offended. We also waste a lot of time and energy.

That's true for me, especially when the insults come from a person I don't like. A good friend will receive patience and grace, but a family member or someone who consistently bugs me . . . I'm almost looking for a reason to get upset.

"But I really can't offend you," said Bishop Joey Johnson of Akron's House of the Lord. "I may say something that bothers you. I may say something that is just plain wrong. But how you feel and react to what I said is up to you."

Can that really be true?

Come on, it's not my fault that someone said something stupid to me.

"That's true," Johnson said, "but why is that some of us are offended more often than others?"

Oh, boy, who wants to answer that question? Especially if it appears we are getting upset more than normal by conversations with friends and family members?

Or even casual contacts with people in stores?

Isn't it easy to think that a clerk is ignoring us because the clerk doesn't respect us or for some other personal reason? And then we can't wait to tell someone about the latest perceived slight.

I know I'm in trouble when I say, "I can't believe he said that to me! That's really offensive."

When I say that, I'm actually taking "a fence."

Imagine walking down a narrow road and coming to a small, rusty fence. I can walk around the fence. Or I can run a few steps and jump over it. While the fence is annoying, I just need a few minutes to deal with it and then leave it behind.

Now picture me picking up the fence and carrying the rusty metal around for a few days. I show it to friends so they can see how this stupid fence was right there, trying to hold me up. The longer I carry the fence, the heavier it becomes. I spend even more time obsessing about it. I seek out more people so they can see how the fence—now *my fence*—torments me.

"You can't really blame me for how you feel," Johnson said. "Feelings are real. They need to be dealt with. But they are our feelings."

Think of a stressed mother who comes home from work, spills milk while taking care of her daughter and screams at the 5-year-old, "Look what you made me do!"

While the child may have been whining and possibly even screaming, she didn't dump the liquid on the kitchen floor. The mother did.

Perhaps you are dealing with an adult sibling who has lost another job. Your brother blames everyone but himself. In the process, he is making you feel guilty because you have a decent career.

But is he causing your guilt?

Really?

How about the adult sister who has the great family? She goes on and on about her wonderful life, knowing that you are going through a divorce and making you feel as if you're a failure. She may believe she's just telling you what's happening in her life, but you believe she's putting you down at a time that your life is falling apart.

Another minefield for me is when I start complaining, "She always . . ." or "He never . . ."

Or these comments:

"She just thinks she's so special because she has a good husband and I don't!"

"He walks around as if he owns the place because he got a promotion and I was passed over."

Think about these comments: In both cases the person didn't say anything. Simply being around us was a reason to be offended.

That means I'm attacking the person, not dealing with the subject.

"I believe no one can hurt my feelings as much as they hurt my pride," said Joe Coffey, a pastor at Hudson Community Chapel. "We are often more angry at the person who said it for a variety of reasons, rather than by what the person actually said."

It can be toxic . . . but also addicting.

I know people whose conversations center on how they got a raw deal on something, or how someone mistreated them. It doesn't take long for me to join the complaint commission with my list of gripes.

Coffey said it's best to concentrate on forgiving the person rather than being stuck on what was said.

Quit asking yourself, "Why would that person say that?"

It's possible the person was simply having a bad day. Few of us know what others are going through.

From friends in retail, I've learned to be patient with a grouchy clerk or waitress.

Simply say, "Looks like you're working hard despite having a hard day."

Most times the worker softens, grateful to be noticed as a person with feelings.

The same is true when someone we know insults us.

It's not easy to say, "I sense you're a little bit tired. How are things?"

But a line like that often defuses the anger.

That's a lot better than saying, "Hey, you talkin' to me? What's with you?"

Proverbs 12:16 reads, "A fool shows his annoyance at once, but a prudent man overlooks an insult."

Not easy to do, but carrying it around is even harder.

16

Shut Up and Listen!

"I know I shouldn't say this, but . . ."

Have you ever said that?

Thought so.

Or as Father Gary Chmura of Cleveland's Our Lady of Peace Catholic Church said, "I've done it, and every time I said that, I regretted it."

He paused.

"I mean, *every* time," Chmura said.

Same with me.

Whenever I start a sentence with "I know I shouldn't say this," something is telling me not to say it.

And something is pushing me to say it: "Go ahead, say it . . . it won't hurt anyone."

But part of me knows something is wrong, or I wouldn't have opened with, "I know I shouldn't say this."

In 1 Kings 19:12-14, the author talks about God speaking to the prophet Elijah, and how God's voice came not as an earthquake or a fire but as a "gentle whisper."

And usually that whisper is telling us *not* to do or say something.

"It's like the Holy Spirit is warning me to stop," said the Rev. Donna Barrett, pastor of Rockside Church in Independence. "But too many times I have said it anyway. Then I know I need to repent."

Repent means to be sorry enough to change . . . or sorry enough to apologize and try to fix the situation.

But how?

Once the words are out of our mouths, they are out. Others have heard them.

If I say something like, "I know I shouldn't say this, but Nancy is getting a divorce because her husband is messing around . . . with her best friend!"

That's a fictional example, but I've said things like that. How do I repair the situation? Do I apologize to Nancy? Her husband? The other woman? All the above?

Do I then tell the people who heard my gossip to forget it? Any chance of that working?

When we say, "I shouldn't say this, but . . ." it's like God is telling us, "Just shut up!"

If we then stop in midsentence, the other person often says, "Come on, you can tell me. I won't tell anyone else."

So then we just say it, knowing it's a bad idea as the words leave our mouths.

"For some of us, knowledge is currency," Chmura said. "We don't have money or big cars, but we do have some inside information. It can bring us attention."

Often it's not a fair, impersonal attack. It's not addressing the action. It's attacking the person's character.

That's why we know we shouldn't say it.

I'm writing this at one of my favorite coffee shops. They sell day-old muffins for a buck. I bought one and it was like a glop of goo. I told the woman behind the counter so she'd know and take care of it. She began checking the muffins on sale.

I didn't scream, "They're selling muffins that are glops of goo, and they are doing it because they want us all to die!"

OK, that's an extreme case, but you get the idea. I knew I

should say something to her about the muffins, but not to everyone else.

One of my challenges after I became serious about my faith in the late 1990s was how to write opinions and be critical without being personal.

I talked to two friends who are pastors . . . and very public figures.

They both said the same thing: "Criticize the action, not the person."

For example, a general manager can make a bad trade but that doesn't make him a low-life or an idiot. So many talk shows about sports and politics are fueled by emotion and name-calling.

More than once I've heard people on the radio say: "Look, I know I shouldn't say this, but you and I know this guy is just a moron."

And they are talking about the president of a team . . . or the country.

I've heard that said about Mark Shapiro, president of the Cleveland Indians. I stopped the person and said, "Look, Mark has made what turned out to be some lousy trades, but he graduated with honors from Princeton. I don't think he's a moron."

And it was something I knew I should say. I was glad I said it during a public question-and-answer session at a place where I was giving a speech.

The New Testament book of James spends most of the third chapter warning about all the trouble that comes from our tongues. In 3:8, James writes, "No man can tame the tongue. It's a restless evil, full of deadly poison."

Obviously, that is not true all the time.

But when we start with, "I know I shouldn't say this," the conversation is likely to take an ugly turn.

Has anyone ever said, "I know I should say this, but Amanda's mother did the most wonderful thing today . . ."?

Far more likely, we'll say, "I know you shouldn't talk about someone's mother this way, but . . . "

Then we trash the mother.

Then there's another problem.

What if someone tells us, "I know I shouldn't say this, but . . . "?

If this were sports, someone should blow a whistle and throw a penalty flag to immediately stop the action.

"I know I should tell people to stop when I hear them say, 'I know I shouldn't say this, but . . .'" Chmura said. "But too often, I don't."

That's because there is a dark side of us that wants to hear the dirt and gossip. It makes us feel superior to someone else.

Christian author and speaker Joyce Meyer has said, "If someone tells me that they shouldn't be saying something, I tell them, 'Then don't say it.' That usually shuts them up."

But it also can come across as being rude, which some of us fear. We don't want to offend the person, even if that person is about to offend someone else by spreading gossip or damaging news.

"It takes courage to get out of that kind of conversation," Barrett said.

A while ago someone began telling me something negative about a public figure whom we both know, and I said, "We know the guy has problems and he's a mess; I really don't need the details. I just feel bad for him."

Then I eased the conversation into another direction.

But I don't always drive on that high road. Too often I'm curious to know what's in the ditch on the side of the road.

Barrett said she has memorized Ephesians 4:29: "Do not let any unwholesome talk come out of your mouths, but only what is helpful for building others up according to their needs, that it may benefit those who listen."

I know I shouldn't say this, but . . .

Too often I don't listen to my own advice—and later wish I had.

STUCK IN THE ELEVATOR WITH THESE PEOPLE CALLED FAMILY

I firmly believe that God leads you to help if you let Him. This morning I read your column and then searched the archives for topics that might help as I pray for family members. I found one titled, "Letting family members 'fix' their own lives." This is a note of thanks to you and a note that, by writing it, helps me. I pray that I continue to allow God to lead me in directions where I can find help and peace.

—Patrick McClain, Olmsted Falls

- 17 -

Dads, Hear This

A pastor was talking to a young couple who had been dating for a while and the relationship was turning serious.

He asked them about their families, and they talked a lot about their mothers and grandparents. He then asked about their fathers. Neither had grown up with their biological father, although they did see him occasionally.

The pastor asked what they knew about their fathers.

The more they talked, the more they realized the men were about the same age . . . had the same type of job . . . and even sort of looked the same.

The couple said they had not spoken at length about their fathers with each other. That often is the case when the father is not in the home. Children—even adult children—develop a "father hole" in their hearts.

That's what Bill Glass calls it.

The former Browns defensive end has been a pioneer in prison ministry for nearly 40 years. He also is a friend, and we've written two books together. But even he had not heard a story quite like the one that was developing as the pastor talked with the couple.

That's because the more the details emerged, the more the pastor had a sick feeling. He knew that man. It was the same man.

And that meant he was the biological father to the young man and woman.

And that meant this relationship had to be cut off.

And that meant yet more collateral damage from a missing father.

*   *   *

When I started doing weekly jail ministry, Glass told me I would see a father and son reunion behind bars.

He was right.

At least three times I've had fathers and sons in the same jail Bible class. Twice they had no idea the other was in that jail. They signed up for the class, saw each other —and then embraced. Since neither was aware the other was incarcerated, it's a safe bet that their relationship wasn't close.

On the third occasion, the father and son had been busted together in a crooked business deal.

According to the Fatherhood Initiative website: "A 2002 Department of Justice survey of 7,000 inmates revealed that 39% of jail inmates lived in mother-only households. Approximately 46% of jail inmates in 2002 had a previously incarcerated family member. One-fifth experienced a father in prison or jail."

My experience is that far more than 20 percent of inmates have had a father in prison at some point. In many cases they are embarrassed to admit it—or they aren't even aware of it because the father has been gone so long.

Or they may not even know their father.

In our weekly jail ministry class of about 25 guys, we go around the room and ask each man to give the first name of his children. If he doesn't have children, he can name nieces, nephews, even a kid from the neighborhood. Then we pray for the children after all the names are called.

At least once a month, a man can't name all of his children.

I will repeat this: At least once a month, a man can't name all of his children.

And at least once a month, a man names all of his kids, but it seems to take more effort than naming the state capitals. The poor guy often is in agony, closing his eyes, touching a different finger as he pulls out a name from his memory bank.

And Lord knows how many children come from how many different women.

With the fathers of about 1.5 million children in prison at any point, it's hard to see these trends decreasing. It doesn't matter if the studies are done by religious or secular groups, or by conservative or liberal think tanks, missing fathers create major problems. Children without fathers are more likely to drop out of high school, more likely to become pregnant while a minor and more likely to have everything from poor grades to eating disorders.

With so many fathers absent, we have so many sons growing up with no idea of what it means to be a father.

I make no claims on being an expert on fatherhood. I have no biological children. Most of my relationships are with other adults. But being active in jail ministry since 1998 has led me to study the subject. I've found that people want me to talk about it when I speak to churches and other faith-based groups.

*   *   *

Before going into a list of suggestions for fathers, here's a personal story.

I was blessed to have a terrific dad. You could count on him to hold a job, to stay sober, to teach the value of hard work and the evils of credit cards. If he said he was going to be somewhere at noon, he was usually there 10 minutes early. In an era when some people grow up with missing fathers or frustrated fathers or fathers who are clueless about what being a father really means, my dad belongs on the Mount Rushmore of fatherhood.

But if there were one area where my dad—and so many of us men—could improve, it's in telling those we love how much they mean to us.

When I would mess up, my dad often would say, "How dumb can you be?"

Exactly how do you answer that question?

Don't try this: "If you think that's dumb, just wait until you see what I do next."

A better approach is Proverbs 10:19: "When words are many, sin is not absent, but he who holds his tongue is wise."

My father believed that compliments were like gold nuggets— you seldom hand them out. Silence about a job meant it was well done because you were expected to do things well.

A few years ago a friend had his daughter and a few of her teammates in his car after they had won a big basketball game. His daughter scored more than 20 points, and her team won. He praised their performance but then said to his daughter, "If you had gone inside more, that girl couldn't stop you from getting to the basket."

All the girls were silent. He could see tears running down his daughter's face. He realized he should have waited a few days to mention this, doing it when he and his daughter were alone.

He had stolen their joy.

We need to be more like parents and friends than coaches. Glass often says that. He means that many coaches never say that a player or a team played a perfect game. A coach's goal is to keep demanding more. It's about performance, not a relationship.

Glass has spent nearly 40 years in prison ministry. His main theme is Deuteronomy 30:19: "I have set before you life and death, blessings and curses. Now choose life so that you and your children may live."

Sometimes we need to hear "You did a good job"—period!

My father didn't know how to praise others. Growing up during the Depression in an immigrant household where English was a distant second, he received little praise. Life was hard, money was short, hunger was real. People needed to shut up and get to work, surrounding themselves with emotional barbed wire. That often made it hard for them to stay close to people.

When angry, my father would call me "Half-a-job Terry." He negated that by taking me to ball games, playing catch in the back yard and being a dad who I knew would always be there. But the label of "Half-a-job" stuck with me, as labels from parents often do.

Children want consistency—not necessarily perfection, although they may act that way at times. But if Dad says he'll be there at 10, he's there at 10. Or he calls to say he will be late.

I've had friends who grew up in homes where their biological fathers had moved out. They loved the idea of spending weekends with their dads. But there were times when dad was hours late, or didn't come at all.

They'd wait and wait and wait.

No one called. Nothing happened. Hearts were broken . . . again.

While my father would never have broken a record for giving compliments, he was like the National Anthem before every game. You knew it was coming, and when it was coming. And there's comfort in that.

What children want from parents—especially fathers—is reliability. It creates a sense of safety. And one can't feel loved unless one feels safe.

*   *   *

Here are some other tips for fathers:

1. You can be a dad even if you aren't in the home. Work to spend time with your kids. And when you do have your children, make sure they feel important. Don't just bring them over and dump them off with your new family's children and expect everyone to get along. Your children need your presence.

2. Cards, emails, texts and calls mean so much, even if the kids

act as if they don't care about receiving them. Research shows that women buy about 75 percent of all cards, so you can be sure that daughters love receiving cards from Dad.

3. When we're not sure whether we should go positive or negative in a situation, go positive. Why? Because we can always go negative later. And if we're negative too early in a relationship, it's hard to recover if we're wrong.

4. When we criticize, be sure to attack the action, not the person. A bad idea doesn't make the person an idiot. Explain why the idea won't work, not why the person is an incompetent nincompoop. Name-calling is toxic.

5. Memorize Proverbs 15:30: "A cheerful look brings joy to the heart, and good news gives health to the bones." When we look for reasons to praise those close to us, it lifts everyone.

6. Be careful with promises. Kids and adult children may forgive a broken promise from Dad, but they still could have trouble forgetting it. Unless you are pretty certain you will do something, it's dangerous to say, "I'll think about it," when a child asks for a favor. To children (and many adults), that sounds like "yes".

7. In Matthew 5:37, Jesus teaches: "Simply let your 'yes' be 'yes,' and your 'no' be 'no.'" Take it one more step. Someone once told me, "It's always easier to go from a 'no' to a 'yes' than from a 'yes' to a 'no.'" When we change from "yes" to "no," we disappoint people.

8. Intentions mean little to spouses and children. They judge us by our actions. I recall an adult woman in tears telling me how her divorced father used to promise to pick her up on weekends but rarely showed up on time. And about half the time, he didn't show up at all. He'd tell the girl he "meant" to get her, but "something came up." He was "really sorry," but his behavior didn't change.

9. Along with keeping his word, a father's greatest gift to his family is his willingness to apologize, especially if it's backed up by not making the same bad decision or stupid remark again.

10. When a father criticizes a teacher, a pastor or a family member, the kids hear every word and take it to heart. It shapes their opinions. Consider that before you speak. And if you want your kids to go to a place of worship, take them—and go to the service with them. The dad who drops the family off at the door, then kills an hour somewhere else before returning to pick them up, sends a mixed message. Young males especially will follow your example.

18

Mothers and Daughters: Heaven Help Us

Marie (not her real name) had a choice. Her boss wanted to know which of two jobs appealed to her most. One position played to the strengths that God gave her, while the other would have been just OK.

To many people, the answer would have been easy. But Marie has never been good at speaking up for herself.

Her relationship with her mother left her terrified of making someone unhappy. It's an issue that can live inside a daughter long after her mother is gone—the fact that some daughters believe it was their job in life to please their mothers.

When Marie was about 10, her parents divorced. She kept in touch with her father and loved spending time with him. But he moved out, remarried and created another family.

Marie's mother had been depressed before the divorce. But afterward she didn't cook much. She didn't clean much. She didn't offer much emotional support. As a teenager, Marie found herself being a mother to her mother, convinced that she had to make up for the pain her mother had endured after the divorce.

Marie knew her parents' relationship had been rocky and her father had left her mother for another woman. But a part of Marie wondered if she had been a "better child," perhaps her parents would have stayed together. Marie's dad remained loving and supportive, but he was in the picture only on some weekends.

When she was 15, her father died of cancer.

And that made her feel even more alone, even more responsible for her mother.

When her father was alive, Marie spent a few weekends each month with him. He made her feel special and protected. She didn't have to worry about his moods. He was a strong presence, even when growing weak from cancer.

Then he was gone.

Marie's mother never directly blamed Marie for the divorce, but she manipulated her with guilt.

When Marie dropped a bag of groceries, for example, her mother raged, "I spent a lot of time at the store. You always do something like this to me."

"Mom," Marie said, "It was an accident."

"No, it's because you're careless," her mother insisted.

To be fair, her mother did bring in enough money so the two of them always had a decent place to stay and enough to eat.

But when her mother would ask what she wanted to do that evening, Marie would reply, "It doesn't matter; you pick."

Of course it did matter, but Marie was afraid to make a choice that would upset her mother.

That fear carried into the rest of her life. Marie worked at pleasing others to such an extent that she lost herself in the process. She was a good student and a good employee because she worked so hard to "get things right."

That was true, even if she wasn't sure she was doing the right thing—she simply was pleasing her teachers, her bosses, her friends.

Marie remained afraid that by simply answering a simple question such as "Do you want pizza or McDonald's?" she'd lose a friendship or a relationship.

It led her to stuff down resentments, making mental lists of unspoken grievances.

Marie didn't grow up with any faith in her life, and only recently has she been considering the idea that there is a God who made her for a special purpose. She still isn't sure about God and what—if anything—that may mean to her life. But she's learning that letting her mother's voice live in her head and rule her life is no way to exist.

I told her about this advice from Kerry Shook, a Houston-based pastor and author: "There are so many people that are glad to tell you what's important and what needs to be done. If you don't decide what's important from the Lord, everyone else will tell you."

When her boss asked which job she wanted, Marie wanted to say, "It doesn't matter that much to me . . ." as if she were still trying to please her mother.

But before the words left her mouth, she thought about what really mattered to her.

And then she expressed a strong opinion about which job was best for her.

Her boss agreed, and she was given the position. She also received more than that.

Marie may always hear her mother's voice rattling around in her brain, but as she told me, "I'm figuring out that what I think matters, too."

It's a battle that may last a lifetime.

The relationships between mothers and daughters "can be complex and not always easy," said Donna Barrett, pastor of Rockside Church in Independence.

I'm not a woman. I don't always understand how women "do" relationships.

Nonetheless, I'm offering up this general statement: Often the relationships between mothers and sons are less complicated. In many families girls tend to think Mom likes the boys better. It's the son who loves to yell, "Hi, Mom!" into the television camera at a game. His emotional challenge often is with his father.

"I know my mother was more nurturing and coddling to my two brothers than to myself and my four sisters," said Diana Swoope, pastor of Akron's Arlington Church of God.

Swoope believes it was because her mother "was preparing us to make a way in a man's world."

When I asked a middle-aged friend named Rhoda to describe mother/daughter relationships, she put her two fists together. It was to demonstrate how both sides easily rub each other the wrong way.

"I think that's often true," said Jan Fillmore, a pastor at Mayfield United Methodist in Chesterland. "It revolves around the question, 'Do I measure up?' Moms worry about having done the right thing in raising their daughters, and daughters worry about meeting the expectations of their mothers."

Sometimes, the mother doesn't like how her grown daughter runs the house, treats the children or handles the money—and her tone makes the daughter feel as if she were a 6-year-old again. Rhoda said some mothers see their lost youth and broken dreams in their daughters—especially if the daughter has the family and the lifestyle that Mom lacked.

Or the daughter may feel she failed because her marriage broke up or one of her children has struggled.

"My mother is 89 and we get along better than ever because we have wanted to make our relationship work," said Rhoda.

According to Swoope, "Sometimes we have this fantasy of what the relationship is supposed to look like. But what happens is after we get older and have children, we find out what our own mothers have dealt with."

If you look deeply at what seems a smooth relationship between a mother and daughter, "You'll find they had some rough times, too," said Swoope. "They just don't show it, or they got over it."

There are times when daughters have to throw some of the mother baggage out of the emotional trunk and drive off, leaving it in the rear view mirror. It's fascinating that one of the Ten Commandments is not "*Love* your father and mother." It's "*Honor* your father and mother."

It's as if God speaking through Moses knew that some parents might be impossible to love.

"We should give thanks to our mothers at least for giving us a start in life," Barrett said. "And we should be thankful to other women who have helped us. In addition to my mother, I've had at least four who have been like mothers to me at different times in my life."

Fillmore said her relationship with her mother "has had its ups and downs." But she said she is so thankful her mother "taught me to read and write . . . she is in her 80s and she continues to encourage me, despite her facing some health issues."

Some experts have suggested mothers and daughters exchange letters as a way to repair the relationship.

"Some of us should ask: What is the real problem? What started it?" Swoope said. "Often it's not a big deal, but people don't talk for years—and it gets worse and worse."

Marie and her mother do talk, several times a week. They have found a common ground (both like to work on the house and in the garden), and doing things together seems to bring more peace. Yes, Marie still finds herself wanting to please her mother and not always telling her, "Mom, it's time to go home," when it's time for them to separate.

"But now when I do say that I have to leave, I don't feel as guilty," Marie said. "I'm not as mad at her as I used to be. It still comes up, but I can see a difference."

19

Is He Really *My Brother?*
Is She Really *My Sister?*

Did you grow up with a jerk for a brother or sister?

This is a faith-based book, so I'm supposed to be kind, patient, understanding and, most of all, long-suffering.

Which is what it's like when there is a sibling who is constantly in trouble, in and out of jail, often broke—and breaking both the hearts and budgets of the family. He crawls home when the money runs out and the fun ends. He knows how to apologize through tears and seems truly dedicated to changing.

And perhaps he will—only he never has before.

"Families can be some very nasty business," said Father Gary Chmura.

The Roman Catholic priest at Our Lady of Peace in Cleveland has talked to people who have been stacking up slights and grievances for "more than 30 years. It's like we nurture them, and they keep growing."

There are stories of a parent favoring one child over another, or of one sibling taking advantage of the others.

"So much of it is perception," Chmura said. "In my family there were five kids. Four of us see things one way. The fifth has a totally different view of how we were raised."

Most parents acknowledge that they don't treat each child the same. Part of the reason is that each child is different. Another factor is that some children are easier to love than others.

"I once read about a mother of 10 children who said her favorite child was the one who was sick—until she was better," Chmura said. "And she said her favorite child was the one who left the family—until he comes back."

The child with troubles or illness soaks up much of the attention from parents who want to "heal" the situation. But it also leads to resentment from the children who don't receive much attention.

If you are the "good" daughter or son, you've known the emotional and financial price the family has paid to help "the prodigal." You know that it can wear out everyone involved. It also can lead to the "good kids" feeling as though they are taken for granted.

That's something rarely mentioned when you hear sermons on Luke 15, the parable of the prodigal son. It's the story of two boys. The older one stays home to help Dad run the farm. The younger takes off with his share of the inheritance. The younger son blows the money and ends up working in a pigpen. Finally he comes home, expecting to be chastised and treated like a slave by his father. But Dad throws a party to celebrate his return. The oldest son refuses to go. Instead, he throws himself a pity party because it seems as though Dad likes the rebel son best.

The typical sermon dismisses the older son as "bitter," a word used a few times in the Luke 15 notes of the *Life Application Bible*. The authors add: "The older brother represents the Pharisees, who were angry and resentful that sinners were being welcomed into God's kingdom. . . . How easy is it to resent God's gracious forgiveness of others whom we consider to be far worse sinners than ourselves."

Take that, you judgmental, self-righteous sons and daughters.

Ever wonder whether those who speak so harshly of the older brother endured a hard-core prodigal in their own family?

The Rev. Bill Buckeye of Bay United Methodist Church in Bay Village said he preached a three-part series on the parable, a part from the view of each son and their father. It changed his understanding of the story.

"To the older son, it seems someone changed the rules, and that's not fair," Buckeye said. "It happens a lot in the workplace. You do your job, are loyal to the company, and they lay you off or pass you over [for a promotion] in favor of someone younger who hasn't done nearly as much."

*   *   *

The first death recorded in the Bible was when Cain murdered Abel, his brother.

Why did he do it?

Because God liked the sacrifices made by Abel better than those of Cain.

Genesis 4:6-7: "Then the Lord said to Cain, 'Why are you angry? Why is your face downcast? If you do what is right, will you not be accepted? But if you do not do what is right, sin is crouching at your door; it desires to have you, but you must master it.' "

But Cain killed Abel.

"It was jealousy," said Rabbi Steven Denker of Temple Emanu El in Orange. "In the family, it's about who got something we wanted. It can be the nuclear family or the human family."

Denker's point is that we usually don't physically harm a family member, but we cut them off from the family. We also can murder their reputation by what we say to family members and friends.

Obviously, in some families there is major physical abuse. I once met a man with scars all over his chest and back. He said his mother hit him with a hot iron. In other families, drugs and alcohol destroy any sense of security. But in many situations, the problem is as old as Cain and Abel—envy.

We have to pray to help us see our family mess through God's eyes, not ours.

I know of some families where one sibling sexually abused the other. I know of families where drug-addicted siblings continually stole from the entire family. In these cases, keeping a distance is imperative. We must forgive them and not dwell on how they have hurt us, but we don't need to allow them complete access to our lives and families.

Too often, though, it's the small things that simply need to be forgotten so we can move on with our lives.

Chmura told of a man who 25 years later was still hurting because his older brother got the new bike and baseball glove while he got the hand-me-downs.

"When you say some of this stuff out loud, it sounds sort of dumb and petty," Chmura said.

But families can snare us in an irrational web of insecurity.

"Families can be the source of our greatest joy and the deepest wounds," said Jeff Bogue, pastor of Grace Church in Akron. "Because we don't pick our families, but we spend so much time with them, it seems the emotions run higher than they do with other people."

After Cain murdered Abel, God asked Cain what happened to his brother.

"I don't know," said Cain. "Am I my brother's keeper?"

Bogue said, "Sometimes emotions lie to us. They color what really happened. They lead us to doing things we never would if we calmed down and thought about it."

We also have to admit that sometimes we want it both ways. We can get stuck on the subject of "fairness." We think someone else in the family received more breaks, more attention, more patience from our parents. Those feelings can remain long after our parents are dead. The fact is, we never can make family relationships "fair" because it's hard for siblings or even spouses to decide what constitutes "fair."

Just as most of us think we are underpaid or underappreciated at work—at least compared with someone else—we can believe that our parents favored the other sibling.

Families often are divided over money. If a relative gives me a loan, I may think, "Because he's related to me, I can pay him last. He'll understand."

But he thinks, "I'm his brother, he should pay me first. Family always comes first."

Rabbi Stephen Grundfast of Akron's Beth El Congregation said, "I have met people who haven't spoken for 50 years over money and business dealings. By now they would have settled the account with a stranger, but because it's family, the resentment lingers."

*   *   *

The split between the two sons in the parable of the Prodigal Son begins over money.

How many of us have said: "She always reacts like that. . . . I knew she'd get into money trouble again."

Or maybe we say: "They always spoiled him when we were kids. Now look at how he behaves."

Bishop Joey Johnson of Akron's House of the Lord said it helps to know the cultural setting during the time that Jesus was telling this story.

When the younger son asked his father to give up the inheritance right now, it was as if he was saying, "I wish you were dead so I could get my money." Jesus' audience could easily relate because many knew what it was like to wait for their own father to die so they could take over the family or business—as they had been working for their father for decades.

But they also knew that asking for the inheritance early was an outrageous insult.

Even more shocking to the audience is when Jesus said the

father "divided his property between [the sons]."

In their tradition, the older son received two-thirds of the estate, with the younger son taking the other third.

"I believe this story said it was 50/50," Johnson said. "No Middle Eastern father would do this."

Johnson also said that the "estate" wasn't just money. It included livestock, land and other holdings. For the younger son to raise the cash needed to travel "to a distant country," he needed to sell these things. That would have made the audience hate the younger son even more, because he was diluting the estate built up by the father.

And no doubt the older son seethed during all this.

The younger son blows all his money and returns home beaten and broke, ready to beg his father simply to be treated as a hired hand.

When the father spots the son, Jesus said, "He ran to his son, threw his arms around him and kissed him."

"Middle Eastern gentlemen do not run in public," Johnson said. "Young boys run; owners of estates do not. . . . One of the main reasons Middle Easterners of rank do not run is that traditionally they have all worn long robes. This is true of both men and women. No one can run in a long robe without gathering the robe into his/her hands . . . Consequently, when one gathers his/her robe to run, the legs are exposed and this is considered humiliating."

Then the father throws a party for the younger son, while the older son pouts and refuses to attend.

Johnson said the younger son should have been exposed to a "qetsatsah ceremony."

According to author Kenneth Bailey (*Finding the Lost: Cultural Keys to Luke 15*), "Angry villagers would gather together to conduct what was known as a ceremony, a ritual that consisted of filling a large pot with burned nuts and burned corn and then breaking it in front of the guilty party. As the earthenware pot shattered, the villagers would shout: 'So-and-so is cut off from his people.' That would be the cue for the errant son to get out of town for good."

But the father welcomes him home.

At this point, the older son would receive all the sympathy from the audience.

But the way he received his father's invitation to the party also was a sign of disrespect.

The audience would have also been shocked when the father left the party to talk to the son.

"No Middle Eastern father would behave this way," Johnson said. "If he did leave the party, the guests would probably accompany the father. They'd expect the servants to tie up his son. Then they'd return to the party. When the banquet was over, the older son would have been beaten."

But the father listens to his older son's complaints. When the older son says, "you have never even given me a young goat so I can celebrate with my friends," most of the audience would know the older son was just whining. The older son has a lot of privilege in that culture. His angry tone in his remarks to his father also would have been seen as nearly as disrespectful as to what the younger son did when he first departed.

"We never should start comparing ourselves with others," Johnson said. "That leads to resentment."

One message from Luke 15 is that no matter how far we wander from God, we can always come back. It's powerful and needed. Another message is that we should welcome those who struggle back into our places of worship.

But the story also opens the door to discussions about family relationships and how to handle not only the troubled son but also the "good kids" of the family. Consider how Jesus ended the parable, speaking to the older son in Luke 15:31-32: "My son," the father said, "you are always with me, and everything I have is yours. But we had to celebrate and be glad, because this brother of yours was dead and is alive again; he was lost and is found."

My guess is that Dad hugged the older son and together they

went to the party. The "good kid" needed to be reassured, something too often ignored in some families. And the father didn't care about the cultural norms of the day; he wanted to keep the family intact.

But notice that both sons—in their own way—came back to the father. They had to take some steps to be restored.

Father Bob Stec of St. Ambrose Roman Catholic Church in Brunswick said: "If we are truthful, sometimes what annoys us in a family member are the same weaknesses and faults that we have, but we don't want to admit it."

That is powerful. In their own way, both sons were selfish, both disrespectful of the father—and both jealous of each other.

Chmura said that when dealing with people who are upset with family members—the anger stretching back years—it helps to have them list specific examples that caused the anger. Not the "Mom likes you best" generalities, but exactly what happened.

"Often, as they work through the list, people realize that many of the things were not a big deal or they happened so long ago," Chmura said. "It's something someone said, or how they like to brag about their kids or their job. If you can put some of the emotion aside, you begin to realize that it really is time to let a lot of this stuff go."

20

Fix This? No Way

I was talking to a woman whose daughter is back in jail after going back on drugs. The mother said she tried to help, letting her daughter move into the house again . . .

The woman couldn't finish the story through her tears.

I told her, "I don't know the details, but I do know this is not all your fault."

Another woman said to me, "I've heard that a mother only feels as good as her worst child is doing."

"I don't think that's fair," I responded.

She stared at me strangely.

"Your child should not be responsible for your moods," I said. "Nor is it fair to your friends and family that you allow a struggling child to drag you down."

She wasn't listening; she was too stuck in her sorrow.

"It can tear your heart up to be waiting for someone to get sober, someone to pull their life together," said Father Damian Ference, a philosophy professor at Borromeo Catholic Seminary. "When I was a young priest, I wanted people to come to church right now. They needed to realize how they were hurting themselves and others."

Ference said the result was "pushing them so hard, it pushed them away."

"It was Pope John Paul II who said we needed to propose things to people, not impose on them," Ference said.

He meant that we can open the door for others, but we shouldn't try to drag them through it. Most people who allow a troubled adult relative to move into their homes really do care about them.

"I recently was talking to a woman whose son is on drugs and he stole a bunch of her stuff and sold it," said Marshall Brandon, a pastor at Hudson Christ Church. "She threw him out of the house. Then let him come back. This time he stole the title to her car, forged her name and sold it. I know other people who let family members move back in and they stole credit cards and ran up huge bills."

Brandon said that in some cases, such people should be turned over to the police. But rarely will family members do that. In fact, they seldom even insist on being repaid.

That leads to more family messes, more resentment.

Brandon is in charge of a Celebrate Recovery program for addicts and their family members. He sees guilt lead people to make horrible financial and personal decisions—all because they want to help someone whose life is worse than any reality show.

"No one had a perfect life growing up," Brandon said. "My father was an alcoholic. But that doesn't mean I have to drink. We all make our own choices."

Brandon is not claiming sainthood. Many years ago he was involved in Youngstown gang life and did jail time.

"There are consequences for bad choices," he said. "If you let someone who used drugs into your house, and they continue to use drugs—only it's now in your house—then it's your fault. I know people whose family members moved in and sold drugs out of the house, and they wouldn't throw the dealer out."

Too often it's an attempt to "fix" something that went wrong in their lives.

"We are afraid to let people own their own mistakes," said

David Loar, pastor of the Fairlawn West United Church of Christ. "By bailing them out, we also don't allow them to own their own accomplishments. Too often we get in the way of what God is doing in their lives."

He means teaching them through pain. Most of us don't change until the pain becomes greater than our fear of change. It's tempting to fall into the trap of believing that because we were divorced—for instance—our adult kids can't hold a job and they have good reason to be angry so often. We forget that many, many kids from divorced homes—and far more dire situations— don't have the same struggles.

"Read the first 11 chapters of Genesis," Loar said. "The families are worse than anything on *Jerry Springer*, and God used all those people. But they had to go through a lot of pain first."

There are countless stories of adult children moving back into the house and turning into 13-year-olds. Mom does the cooking and cleaning, and pays for everything. That 30-something child may not be on drugs or into crime. He or she is just stuck, not doing much of anything. And the family may allow them to stay in that adolescent limbo.

"If you are bringing an adult family member in your house, set goals and standards," said Brandon. "They have to get a job—any kind of job. They have to pay rent. They have to clean up. They have to go to meetings at church if they have addiction problems. Or they have to get counseling. They have six months or a year, a set time frame, to get out on their own. And if they don't stick to the rules, they are kicked out. Tough love is just that—tough," said Brandon. "But in these cases, it often is the only real love, because nothing else will work."

Mike Conklin is pastor of Hudson's Rejoice Lutheran Church. But once upon a time he was laid off from his job at Ford. His mother worked at a local church. Still, no matter what she said or did, he was done with church.

He said: "One day the pastor came by. It was about 11 in the morning, and I'd just gotten up. I was living with four other guys. . . . I invited him in and cleared the beer cans off the couch. I asked if he wanted to sit down and offered him some cold pizza sitting on the table."

The pastor passed on the pizza, remained standing and simply said, "We'd like for you to come back to church."

The pastor didn't stay long. There was no lecture, just an open invitation.

"I knew my mother sent him," said Conklin. "But a few weeks later I went back to church. I had hair down to my shoulders. I wore jeans. I figured people would reject me, but they welcomed me back."

That started a long road that eventually led him to entering the ministry.

"Too often we want to dump all our spiritual knowledge on people," said Jonathan Schaeffer, pastor of Grace Church in Middleburg Heights. "We are so desperate for them to change, we figure if they just knew what we knew."

One of the worst things to say is: "If I were in her position, I know I'd do it this way. . . ."

But we are not that person or in the same situation.

We often need to just wait.

"St. Monica prayed for 32 years for her son," Ference said. "And there was St. Augustine, who battled lust and so many other problems. But who wants to wait and pray in a culture that insists we shouldn't have to wait for anything?"

I know someone who is waiting for an aging parent to stop gambling. I know two middle-aged children who've had family interventions to persuade a parent to stop drinking. One worked, one did not. There are countless parents who wonder if their adult children will ever stop bringing so much pain on themselves and others.

Psalm 130:5 reads: "I wait for the Lord, my soul waits, and in his word I put my hope."

Schaeffer suggested we quit worrying so much about how a troubled family member "makes us look." He means how those troubles could affect our reputations.

"It's not easy when someone we care about is way off track," said Schaeffer. "But if we walk around with a long face and make them know how miserable we are when we see them . . . they probably won't change."

All the pastors talked about praying for patience, not just with another person, but also with ourselves. We can't change anything about them, but we can do something about our attitude.

"And that may help bring them back," Ference said.

21

The Spice of Life

He came to live with Gloria not long after her father died.

Gloria was in her 30s. Her mother and father had split up years before. She had lived with her dad; her brothers lived with her mother.

These things happen, as many families know. But now Gloria was living alone for the first time in her life.

And she was terrified.

That's when her mother, Melva, sent a special roommate.

Spice was part collie and part Rottweiler—and entirely devoted to Gloria.

Melva had trained him, and he was smart. When Gloria passed out one day, Spice woke her up. When a couple of strange guys approached her on the street, Spice chased them away even though they outweighed him by more than 100 pounds. He became her best friend, her protector, the one she knew would always have time to listen to her.

Gloria called Spice "the angel dog."

Melva used to say, "The way that dog looks at you, it's just like your daddy did."

It was that way for 18 years. That's right, Spice lived to be 18—something like 126 in human years. Some of Gloria's friends said Spice was the Methuselah of dogs. Methuselah, an Old Testament patriarch, lived to be 969, according to the book of Genesis. So it's not surprising that Gloria believed Spice would always be there, right up until she decided to take Spice to the vet for the final time.

He had stopped eating and was in pain, no longer happy to see her or anyone else.

For more than a year, Gloria had cared for Spice even though he could no longer walk. She fed him Cesar dog food from a spoon. She papered part of her house with puppy pads and constantly changed them to keep him clean. When Spice developed bed sores, she cleaned and treated them.

That's the role reversal from Luke 16:20-21: "At [the rich man's] gate was laid a beggar named Lazarus, covered with sores and longing to eat what fell from the rich man's table. Even the dogs came and licked his sores."

Gloria can't count how many times God used Spice to bring emotional healing.

As Psalm 147:3 reads: "God heals the brokenhearted and binds up their wounds."

Spice never looked at Gloria as if she were stupid. He did seem perplexed by what she was doing sometimes and stared at her with his head tilted, his eyes questioning.

She never had to worry about Spice laughing at her. There were times, however, when they seemed to laugh together when he jumped on the couch to cuddle next to her.

There is so much truth in the prayer, "Lord, help me to be the person that my dog thinks I am."

For 18 years, Gloria never came home to an empty house. Spice was there, waiting. There is real comfort in that.

For those who have never had a treasured pet, all of this may sound like sentimental slop. But the millions who know that God sent dogs, cats, horses and other pets to earth to give us a taste of heaven can understand how people like Gloria feel when they must make that final decision about the animals they love.

Moses said in Deuteronomy 31:6: "Be strong and courageous. Do not be afraid or terrified because of them, for the Lord your God goes with you; he will never leave you nor forsake you."

That remains true, even after losing a close friend like Spice.

*   *   *

Is that it? Will we never see our friends again?

Or will our pets be in heaven?

My wife is counting on it.

Like some of us, she finds it easier to relate to animals than people. Her favorite job was working on horse farms, but she battled allergies and eventually had to quit. Her allergies also forced her to give up having cats as pets at home.

Animals in heaven?

"John Wesley, the founder of Methodism, believed that he would be reunited in heaven with the horse that had been his faithful traveling companion for more than two decades," said Rev. Scott Wilson, pastor of Mayfield United Methodist Church in Chesterland. "Having experienced the love of a number of pets in my life (even though the Bible gives no specific indication), I would not be surprised if they were near the front of the line to greet me when I get there."

Rev. Wilson and other religious leaders mentioned Isaiah 65:25: "'The wolf and the lamb will feed together, and the lion will eat straw like the ox, but dust will be the serpent's food. They will neither harm nor destroy on all my holy mountain,' says the Lord."

That verse seems to hint of animals being in heaven.

"I am convinced there will be animals," said Rev. Donna Barrett, pastor of Rockside Church in Independence. "Animals were an important part of God's Creation. He directed Noah to take them on the ark, two by two. God had a plan to save animals. Part of heaven is that we get the desires of our hearts, and for many of us, that includes animals."

Genesis 1:25 reads: "God made the wild animals according to their kinds, the livestock according to their kinds, and all the creatures that move along the ground according to their kinds. And God saw that it was good."

God created animals because he liked animals . . . after all, God said they were "good."

One theory is that there will be different forms of life in heaven, with angels being an example of something not fully like the human soul.

Gloria insisted Spice was part angel. Who knows whether that's true? But it's easy to see something special in certain dogs, cats, horses and other animals.

*   *   *

The presence of animals in eternity is open to debate. Rabbi Stephen Grundfast of Akron's Beth El Congregation said, "Animals don't have souls, so it's hard to know if they will be in the afterlife. I'd tend to say not."

But he also said there was no way to know for certain.

"I don't know, either," said Father Walt Jenne of St. Basil Catholic Church in Brecksville. "Some theologians would say there are no souls in animals, so they won't be in heaven. But I also think there is a spirit about animals that is not the same as the human soul but could still mean they are in heaven."

Father Jenne said he blessed a friend's sick dog, and his associate pastor has blessed animals on the feast of St. Francis.

"I was visiting someone at Fairview Hospital and ran into a man in a wheelchair," Father Jenne said. "He had a dog with him and said the dog was his best friend. I can understand that. I had dogs growing up, and I really grieved each time one died."

Billy Graham, the nationally known evangelist, answered a question about pets in heaven on his Web site by first saying that he has had many pets and then explaining: "God will provide us with everything we need to be happy in heaven—and if animals are necessary to make us completely happy there, then you can be confident He will arrange for them to be with us."

"Bible Answer Man" Hank Hanegraaff, writing on his Web site (OnePlace.com), voted for animals in heaven:

"First, the Garden of Eden was populated by animals, thus there is a precedent for believing that Eden restored will also be populated by animals. . . . Throughout the history of the church, the classic understanding of living things has included the doctrine that animals, as well as humans, have souls. . . . Finally, while we cannot say for certain that the pets we enjoy today will be resurrected in eternity, I am not willing to preclude the possibility. Some of the keenest thinkers—from C.S. Lewis to Peter Kreeft—are not only convinced that animals in general, but that pets in particular, will be restored in the resurrection."

Revelation, the final book in the Bible, is full of poetry, symbolism and prophecy. In Chapter 19, the author writes about "the armies of heaven riding on white horses." In the book "Heaven," Christian author Randy Alcorn makes the case for animals in the afterlife. His point is that just because animals don't have human souls—and just because Jesus didn't die for the sins of animals— they still may have souls of another type. And if heaven in some way mirrors the Garden of Eden, there will indeed be animals."

I've never heard a sermon about animals in heaven. Most religious leaders seem to dismiss this topic as trivial.

But as Father Jenne said, "It's close to the heart of a lot of people. It does matter, and we should talk about it."

Reader Chip Hautala emailed this:

> I used to laugh at my wife when we were first married because she took in every stray and found it a good home. She's taken me on adventures to rescue a horse from a dog food factory, driven halfway across Ohio to take a litter of kittens someone dumped to a non-kill shelter and fostered many dogs and cats. She has been known to even stop her car in traffic to help a

turtle get across the road! I think she rubbed off on me because I began to appreciate that animals do have a purity of spirit.

The lick on the face and look of unconditional love from your dog after a bad day of work . . . it's better than any therapy or tonic. It's a spiritual reminder of what Jesus Christ tells us every day of our lives and that lick on the hand brings me closer to God than any Sunday service. I just can't imagine a world without dogs; they are a blessing from above."

I like this from Peter Kreeft, a philosophy professor at Boston College and author of many books on faith:

"Is my dead cat in heaven? Again, why not? God can raise up the very grass, why not cats? Though the blessed have better things to do than play with pets, the better does not exclude the lesser. We were meant from the beginning to have stewardship over the animals. . . . It seems likely that the right relationship with animals will be part of heaven: proper 'petship.' And what better place to begin than with already petted pets?"

WHEN HOLIDAYS AREN'T HAPPY

I love reading your faith articles ... the one from Easter was really good and it brought back childhood memories about growing up with my parents, too. Funny, in my case it was always my father who was "late" and my mom was always on time. Keep up the great work.
—Linda LaPinta, South Euclid

22

Second Chances, Part I

Every time I hear the Christmas song that screams, "It's the most wonderful time of the year," I want to yell back, "Maybe for you!"

That's because I battle the Christmas blues. I end up spending too much time looking in life's rear-view mirror, thinking back to holiday gatherings when relatives argued. Clearly, it was not that way every year or every visit. Most of the relatives got along reasonably well.

But little things, such as presents and when to visit each side of the family, could become big issues. My parents often would engage in a verbal duel even before the car left the driveway. My father believed in arriving 10 minutes early for everything. My mother thought being 15 minutes late counted as "on time."

So my dad would sit in the driveway, car running, temper building, while my mother remained in the bathroom, getting dressed.

"Glory to God in the highest, and on earth, peace . . ."

As I write this, it all sounds so petty. At least I had decent parents. And they did care about me. Many of my friends would have loved to have been in my family. Those holiday clashes are at least 35 years old. Why do they still make me dread the get-togethers? Isn't it time for me to give it a rest?

That's especially true since my wife had a tremendous Thanksgiving gathering at our house with friends and relatives, and she's planning to do the same for Christmas. I know it will be another good day, at least if I act like a grown-up instead of a middle-aged brat.

My wife recently told me how her late father made Christmas fun. He'd play a recording of *A Christmas Carol*, Scrooge's story, as they decorated the tree with ornaments that had special meaning to the family. They'd go to church. The dinner was superb; gifts were exchanged. People liked being with one another, instead of sitting around waiting for someone to say something that would offend them.

Then she married Scrooge.

I'm writing this because those of us who claim to be Christians can lose the power of our faith in the squabbles over shopping and old family feuds. At least for me, it's so easy to forget that Christmas is when Jesus was born in a barn to parents who had their lives turned upside down by events out of their control. It's when street people (the shepherds) were the first visitors. It's when Mary and Joseph had to feel real pressures, fears and doubts about their futures.

It's also when God set events in motion so we could be forgiven for our sin, a word that really means selfishness. It's when we can draw upon supernatural power to forgive others—or at least to be civil at dinner.

Or as Cleveland Catholic Auxiliary Bishop Roger Gries has often preached on Christmas: You still matter to God.

God sent his son Jesus to Earth not because you have a good job. Not because you have money in your 401(k). Not because of anything you have done.

"It's because of the love of God for us," Gries said. "Right now a lot of people are not feeling very loved."

That happens when a layoff notice arrives with the Christmas cards. It happens when what seemed like a safe, smart investment disappears. It happens when a spouse or parent dies and leaves you alone for the holidays. It happens to everyone at some point.

It happens for me because holidays tend to dig up the old family trash.

"It happens when you get older," said the Rev. Ronald Fowler of the Arlington Church of God in Akron.

He told the story of visiting a nursing home during Christmas and kissing a resident on the forehead.

"Her eyes were closed, but she called me by name," he said. "I asked her, 'How did you know it was me?' She said, 'Who else would kiss an old woman?'"

"Anyone who is wise," Fowler said.

I need to remember that Christmas is not about me but about what God has done for me.

It's about Jesus coming to Earth and about the shepherds, the first people called to visit the baby. Many Nativity scenes show a young couple with a newborn baby in a stable that looks like a room at the Hampton Inn. The shepherds who visit are well dressed and everyone is clean. The cows are cute and well groomed.

But Jesus was born in a cave that served as a barn. It smelled like a barn. It had bugs like most barns, with straw that livestock used for beds. There was no indoor plumbing, no heat, nothing but the damp, dark night.

Luke Chapter 2 states that the shepherds were "living in the fields" when an angel appeared to them, announcing the birth of the Messiah.

The shepherds felt rejected by the religious elite because they were not allowed to worship in the main area of some temples. On those rare Sabbaths when they came to town, they had to stay outside in the temple courtyards because of their dirty clothes.

Yet they heard the news first. And they came, drawn by the love of God, the hope that this time they would be accepted.

Gries said that some of us become so tied up with our jobs that when the job is gone, we feel lost and worthless.

Or when we are heavily invested in our families but a spouse leaves—even if it's not our fault—we still have a sense of failure.

Or someone close to us dies and we feel that part of us also went to that grave.

"Jesus came to Earth for us to have a relationship with God, for us to have our sins forgiven," Gries said. "He came to give us a sense of peace because he knows this is not a peaceful place."

Christmas is about healing, about second chances. It's about God reaching down to lift us up, even if we feel as if we're scraping the bottom right now. It's why Jesus spent so much time with the rejected, the sinners, the poor and the widows.

"Jesus doesn't ask what we do for a living," Fowler said, "but who are we in relationship to God? I see this as a time of renewal, a time not to write off people but to give them another chance."

And to leave behind the old family mess that people like me have dragged into the holiday far too many times.

23

Christmas at the Waffle House

At least twice I have had Christmas supper at the Waffle House. Both times it was in the mid-1990s, when I was taking care of my father. He had suffered a stroke and could not walk, talk or use his right arm.

He lived in Florida, and he was much like Dustin Hoffman in the movie *Rain Man*. My father liked everything to be in its place. He'd freak out if the towels were stacked in a different spot, or if his favorite Tribe warm-up suit (He had a couple that were identical) was not clean and ready each morning.

He liked to eat the same foods every day. Breakfast was scrambled eggs, puffed rice and Monks' Bread raisin toast. He had a light lunch, a sandwich and maybe some chicken soup. His favorite dinner was pork chops, sweet potato fries and green Jell-O with fruit. Dessert was coconut cream pie. We always went to a Sarasota restaurant called Der Dutchman.

But on Christmas, Der Dutchman wasn't open. Waffle House was, because Waffle House is always open.

As I write this, it's been 14 years since my father died, but I still remember his diet.

I also remember a doctor telling me that the diet was "bad for him, too much cholesterol."

I stared at the doctor for a while and then said, "The guy can't talk. He can't walk. He can't dress himself. He can't even go to the bathroom by himself. And you're worried about his cholesterol? Eating is one of the few things he still enjoys—I don't care what he eats."

The doctor shrugged and then mumbled that he understood.

I didn't know or care if he did. I just knew that I wasn't going to worry about my father having another stroke at the expense of forcing him to eat food that he absolutely hated. Not when he had suffered so much already.

The doctor probably would have had a stroke if he knew how often I took my father to the Waffle House.

My father liked Waffle House because he could watch the cook cracking eggs, flipping omelets and dropping bacon to sizzle on the grill. It was only after I starting volunteering in prison ministry that I realized that the cook had some serious jailhouse tattoos. What mattered was that he was a nice guy who'd smile and wink at my dad as he worked the grill. My dad would point at him and laugh.

My dad also could point to what he wanted on the menu because it had pictures. The stroke had robbed my dad of the ability to read, although he pretended that he still could.

So we went to the Waffle House for Christmas night bacon, eggs and waffles. We were there with a couple of weary policemen, a few orderlies from a nearby hospital and some others who, like us, had wandered in because they didn't want to be at home alone.

We didn't feel sorry for ourselves. Going to the Waffle House was our own Christmas party.

When it came to Christmas, there was so little that I could give my father. No books to read, no clothes to wear.

He liked his Cleveland Indians shirts, be it a T-shirt or a sports shirt with a collar. He wore sweatpants because they were easy to put on and take off with his one good arm. He had tennis shoes with straps rather than laces. His favorite activities were watching sports on television or playing a card game called "Greek rummy" with anyone who would spend time with him.

Because of the stroke, he couldn't deal the cards. He couldn't hold the cards; we had a small rack for him to stand them up. This man who could figure out bowling averages and batting averages in his head now struggled with the most basic math.

So if he wanted the Waffle House, I wanted the Waffle House.

At that point in my life, the Christmas story meant little to me. I went to church with the same enthusiasm as brushing my teeth or using deodorant. I just wanted to wipe out the stink, but I didn't believe it had any real impact on my life. This was nearly 20 years ago, and when I took my dad to his old church, the only space they had for someone like him in a wheelchair was a back corner. He felt rejected, and we never went back.

That has changed at most churches now. If not, the pastors and leaders should make sure that it does. I know that if someone who knew our situation back then had invited us to church, it would have made a difference.

But at the Waffle House, it seemed everyone was welcome on Christmas night:

Those who had given up on church.

Those who had gone to church early but had to work at night.

Those with no real family or friends.

Those who were working at the Waffle House so their friends could have the day off and be with family.

In the Christmas story, Jesus was born in a barn—actually a cave where animals lived. His first visitors were shepherds, who always had to work and stay with the sheep. As it says in Luke 2:8: "And there were shepherds living out in the fields nearby, keeping watch over their flocks at night." Good hygiene doesn't come from "living out in the fields." The shepherds were so undesirable that they were banned from some temples.

But they were welcomed on the first Christmas, just as my father and I were welcomed at the Waffle House.

Places such as Cleveland's City Mission or the Haven of Rest in Akron continue to welcome all. So do houses of worship that are working hard to open their doors to the whole community.

At some point in our lives, all of us are like the shepherds. We are waiting for an invitation to church, an invitation to dinner, an invitation into someone's life so we can feel some of God's love.

- 24 -

Moments That Try the Soul

"My soul is overwhelmed with sorrow to the point of death."

That's what Jesus said to his closest friends the night before he was arrested and executed. He asked them to keep him company, to pray with him, to steady him.

"My soul is overwhelmed with sorrow to the point of death," he said.

For whatever reason, I didn't remember that line from the religion classes of my youth. I remembered how Peter, James and John fell asleep on Jesus. I remembered how Jesus prayed three times, and how in one account He even "sweated blood."

But not the utter despair of Matthew 26:38.

"My soul is overwhelmed with sorrow to the point of death."

That's one of my favorite Bible verses, which probably says something scary about me. I share that line with friends who are depressed and overwhelmed. They know they are people of faith and they tell themselves, "God is on the throne, so I shouldn't feel like this, right?"

Well, Jesus did.

And if anyone was sure God was on the throne and what that meant, it was Jesus.

There are times—those Garden of Gethsemane moments in

hospital beds and waiting rooms, in courtrooms and lonely bed-
rooms—when we feel our souls being overwhelmed to the point
of death.

Not long after Mother Teresa died, some of her letters became
public. In them she talked about feeling distant from God.

"The silence and the emptiness is so great," she wrote to her
spiritual adviser. "I look and do not see.... Listen and do not hear
. . . the tongue moves [in prayer] but does not speak. . . . I want
you to pray for me—that I let Him have [a] free hand."

Time magazine cited that quote a few years ago in a story
about Mother Teresa's "crisis of faith."

Other writers used her doubts about what God was doing—or
even if God was paying attention—to dismiss her faith entirely.
Some even hinted that she was a bit of a phony because while she
seemed so upbeat in her public appearances, it was a different
story in the dead of night—at least based on some of her letters.

We don't know what triggered Mother Teresa's despair, but it's
not hard to guess. Her ministry in India was to care for the poor,
the forgotten, the sick, and finally, the dying. In her world, a success was "a good death," one where the dying person didn't feel
too alone or in too much pain.

Is there anyone who can do that year after year and not have a
Gethsemane moment?

Or a Gethsemane month?

I received an email from Sam (not his real name):

> My wife left me. She told me that she stopped loving me
> years ago AND that her heart told her it was time to go. . . . I
> wish I could make a deal with God: "I'll give myself to you if you
> give my wife back to me."

A woman sent me this email about the first Easter after her
husband died:

> When you marry, two become one. When one goes to be with
> the Lord, you are torn in two . . . I'm still my own person, but
> half of me is missing.

I thought of these stories when reading Matthew's account of the Easter story of Jesus in the Garden of Gethsemane.

Jesus knows he's about to be arrested. He knows that his father in heaven has asked him to die on the cross. He asks his friends to pray, but Peter, James and John fall asleep three times. Matthew wrote in Chapter 26, verses 37-38: "[Jesus] began to be sorrowful and troubled. Then he said to them, 'My soul is overwhelmed with sorrow to the point of death. Stay here and keep watch with me.' "

But his friends remain asleep, and after three requests through prayer, Jesus accepts God's will—to be crucified.

When Mother Teresa wrote, "The silence and emptiness is so great," she seems to echo the feelings of Jesus in the garden. She asks her adviser to pray for her, just as Jesus asked his friends. And just as Sam asked me in his email.

Real honest-to-God faith is raw and uncensored. It's King David writing in Psalm 142: "Look to my right and see, no one is concerned for me. I have no refuge, no one cares for my life."

Tony emailed about how through prayer he and his wife moved from asking "Why us?" when their child was born with Down syndrome to recognizing "God has blessed us."

Tony wrote: "Not many regular kids who would say, in the middle of the day; 'Papa, let's pray for So-and-So' . . . then sit and fold his hands in prayer. Or, 'Papa, I think Mama needs a hug' (especially if Mama and I have had words). . . . He also told the principal she had a nice butt!"

Tony put a smile on his struggles, but they are real . . . and they are with us . . . every day.

That's a little like Jesus in the garden, praying three times that he would not have to face the cross and the pain. He seemed to know that heaven awaited, that he had a mission and that it was worth the agony.

Still, he felt anxious and fearful, at least at first. Eventually his prayer moved from "My will be done" to "Thy will be done."

When my father had a stroke that disabled him and robbed him of his speech, I prayed for a miracle. Then I prayed that he would die quickly, so that he would not endure a silent life in a wheelchair with so much of his old life gone. And, selfishly, I wanted it over because it made my life harder.

After a year neither prayer had been answered the way I wanted.

Someone once told me, "Prayer often does not change the situation, but it does change how we think and feel about it. So keep praying."

I began to pray, "OK, God, get me through this."

It's a prayer I've heard from cancer patients, parents of adult children who are having problems and people who have lost a job, a spouse, even hope.

About four years after my father's stroke, I finally was living in "Thy will be done" territory. I figured I might as well go along with what God was doing because it was not about to change. My father died six months later, and those were the best six months we had ever had.

On the surface nothing had changed. Inside, I had.

Some Christians love to talk about "the breakthrough," a time when a life dramatically changes. But it often takes heartbreak to get there.

For every Easter Sunday, we have a personal Good Friday, and before that, a Thursday night in the garden.

- 25 -

Second Chances, Part II

Growing up, I never liked Easter.

That's because it always highlighted the rift between my parents—two people who may have once loved each other but who no longer seemed to like or have much in common with the other. Easter meant that my mother would go to church with my father and me. It also meant that she would be 15 minutes late, because she was 15 minutes late for almost everything.

By the time I was born my mother had pretty much given up on church, other than on Christmas and Easter. And my father didn't like going to church on the holidays because the pews were packed—and we'd show up late because of my mother.

My father was chronically early. He would have me in the car about 10 minutes before we were supposed to leave. We would sit in the driveway, my father behind the wheel, the motor running, while I pressed against the back seat, hating what I knew would happen next. When my mother came out of the house and slid into the front seat next to my father, they'd either:

- Argue about being late, and then begin to drag up old feuds from even before I was born.
- Sit and stare straight ahead, not saying a word. You had a feeling the windows would crack from the tension.

When we finally arrived at church, no one in the family was ready to sing, "Christ the Lord is risen today . . . Alleluia!"

I'm not writing this for sympathy. I was blessed with parents who loved me far more than they loved each other. They never took out their frustrations on their youngest child. If only they had been half as kind to each other as they were to me, they would have been much happier. It wasn't until I became an adult that I realized how few of my friends knew that they had both parents who were "there" for them.

My parents believed in me, even if they didn't believe and trust each other.

I wish that back in those days, when we finally did get to church, they had caught even part of the Easter message.

Over the years I've learned that God doesn't show up in the way we think.

That went back to the first Easter, when there was far more turmoil than anything I had experienced.

Jesus had died on the cross. Mary Magdalene and other women went to his tomb because they wanted to pay their last respects and prepare the body for a final burial. The tomb was a cave with a rock in front. In the 20th chapter of John, Mary was weeping after finding the tomb empty. Everyone else from the group had left.

She went back into the tomb, spotting someone she believed was a gardener, and said: "They have taken the Lord out of the tomb, and we don't know where they have put him!"

How many of us have gone looking for God and have come away with an empty feeling? Or like Mary, we don't see God because of our tears and grief?

Looking into the rear-view mirror of my life, I realize that I was Mary on Easter. The anxiety and anger that surrounded our trips to church made the service feel as empty as the tomb that she found that Sunday morning.

And Mary was too upset to figure out what had happened.

"We have to press on to connect with God," said the Rev. Donna Barrett, pastor of Rockside Church in Independence. "God does not always show up where and how we think."

As Mary talked to the man she thought was a gardener, she discovered he was Jesus.

"Sometimes, we don't realize God is there with us because we are hurting," Barrett said.

Forget my family situation for a moment. We can show up at a church service and may even enjoy the songs, prayers and the sermon but still miss all that God has for us.

Father Walt Jenne of St. Basil the Great Catholic Church in Brecksville said that the core message of Easter is redemption. He said that Jesus died on the cross for our sins. In the Old Testament, most ceremonies involved killing animals and spilling blood in order to atone for sin. Something had to die. If not animals, then crops were burned.

Jesus' death on the cross was the ultimate sacrifice for sins.

But Jenne said that we can "know" this but not feel it. We can hear the Easter story over and over, and feel like Mary, staring at the empty tomb of a broken career, of relationships lost or the feeling of health slipping away.

It's hard to follow Mary's lead on this, to keep praying and waiting for God when all we want to do is cry.

Or in my case, I just wanted the service to be over and for my parents to get home and get past whatever they were fighting about.

It's tempting to run as far as possible from God. We may see God as the male authority in our lives who doesn't forgive, who seems to judge everything we do or say. It can be a challenge to separate a heavenly father from an earthly father.

Or Easter may simply be a time when families pull apart rather than come together—and no one even considers the idea of forgiveness. That means change and apologizing, which is scary for most of us.

"Getting close to God sometimes means getting past our fears," said Joe Coffey, pastor of Christ Community Church of Hudson. "Love does conquer fear."

Added Barrett: "That means getting to know who God is and how God wants to connect with us."

Christians believe Easter is about second chances. About forgiveness. About Jesus not left dying on the cross but Jesus breaking free of the grave and the spiritual death that comes from selfishness, such as clinging to old grudges.

I'm sure that there were pastors who spoke about those themes on Easter, but my parents didn't hear it.

By the time they arrived at church, they were so angry at each other that it didn't matter what the pastor said. He could have read from dictionary, starting with the letter Q. Or he could have talked about the 20th chapter of John.

Either my parents missed the good news or they had no interest in applying it.

It was as if the little stones of past hurts had piled up and cemented together into a massive boulder that neither person wanted to move. I wish they could have prayed together—something that my wife and I do every day, either in person or on the phone. Praying together breaks down so many of the petty and selfish walls that can divide us.

I wish my mother and father had not turned Easter into their own little holy war. I wish they had given each other as much grace and mercy as God gives us because that could change so much in so many families.

WHAT WE NEED TO KNOW ABOUT MARRIAGE

Your columns inspire me to be a better person and also introduce me to ideas that broaden my view of our world and people. Today the message was so simple and a great reminder. I will do my best to remember to "be kind."

—Cindy Webster, Madison

26

I Do . . . Even When I Don't

This list about marriage began with an email from a reader whose son's marriage was in trouble. Whenever I write about relationships, some readers are quick to point out that I'm a sportswriter—so what do I know?

Of course, many sports fans insist I don't know anything, or at least not as much as they do.

And more than a few athletes have reminded me that I never played their sport at a high level, so how can I write about it?

Well, my wife and I were married in 1977 . . . and we're still married. We have never come close to divorce, and we have stuck through the times and the strains that could have broken us apart. So while I'm a sportswriter, I also can say that when it comes to marriage, Roberta and I have experience.

Most of our friends have divorced at least once. Many are staggering through destructive relationships. It's heartbreaking to see so many hurting people. In many cases, a breakdown in communication led to the marriages being destroyed.

Too many men are not good listeners. Our conversations often are a means to relay information, not an attempt to understand what the women in our lives are really thinking and feeling.

Most troubled marriages need at least short-term professional help. Most people won't bother to seek it. They'll go to a doctor for a fractured foot but not for something that threatens to break apart their lives.

These observations don't deal with major issues such as abuse, addictions and adultery. But maybe a few of our suggestions will help you.

1. Every marriage is based on something besides love. What is yours based on? Security? Money? Sex? Fear of being alone? Children? Convenience? Most couples never bother to ask this question. Have guts enough to ask it.

2. Jesus said a house must be built on rock, not on sand. That's because sand can be washed away when trouble comes (Matthew 7:24-27). What is your marriage built upon? How do you make decisions?

3. Here are three potential problem areas: sex, money and communication. The biggest is communication. If communication breaks down, the relationship can explode. Or it can become an uneasy business partnership with most of the discussion revolving around the kids and the daily schedule.

4. Do we really need five credit cards? Pastor Rick Warren of Saddleback Church in California often asks, "Are you buying stuff you really don't need just to impress people you really don't like?" Money problems are bigger than any elephant in the room because they follow you into every room and into every family relationship.

5. Discuss every major financial decision. Then pray about it. Even after you've reached a conclusion as a couple, wait at least a day before doing it. No one has to buy a car or a house on the spot. And, please, don't rush out and buy something from an infomercial because "time is running out."

6. Your spouse can't make you happy. You are responsible for your contentment. We spend so much time praying for God to change the other person. How about praying that God changes you?

7. Look to how you can help your spouse, rather than pouting

about him/her not helping you. Quit keeping score. Scorekeepers always think they win, but they usually make the situation worse. Besides, when we're in the scorekeeping stage of a relationship, do we really think we are playing fair? Who gets the benefit of the doubt?

8. Criticize the action, not the person. Saying, "It was a bad idea when you knew you were late and didn't call me," works so much better than yelling, "You never call. You're always late. You don't care about me. There's something really wrong with you. Why do you always act this way?"

9. You'll never make a point using the words "never" or "always" because the other person will find the exception.

10. Pray together. Do it out loud. Hold each other's hands. Pray from the heart; don't say some quick, worn-out prayers. Don't turn prayers into accusations.

11. Finally, get into the same ministry together—visit hospital patients, help handicapped kids, find something you can do as a couple to honor God. Sometimes couples grow apart for a simple reason: they stop doing things together. Not just eating out . . . I mean doing things, from sports to charities.

27

What Men Need to Know

What do women want from men?

Probably more than I'll ever know, being a man. Whenever I've talked about male-female relationships, I've had some readers criticize me for being:

A. Too general.

B. Too stereotypical.

C. Too much a clueless sportswriter.

As one reader (unsigned) emailed:

> Thanks for perpetuating the idea that men and women are SO different that we will never be able to understand each other, and the only way men can get along with women is to make us feel important by listening to us talk. It's this juvenile, chauvinistic attitude that ensures many men and women will never truly understand each other.

OK, so men shouldn't even bother to listen to women? What is the alternative?

Besides, "He doesn't listen to me" is one of the most common complaints women have about the men in their lives—be it husbands, brothers, sons, friends or bosses.

The author of *His Needs, Her Needs*, Dr. Willard Harley, wrote in *New Man* magazine: "The most common reason women give for leaving their husbands is 'mental cruelty.' When legal grounds for divorce are stated, about half report they have been emotionally abused. But the mental cruelty they describe is rarely the result of their husband's efforts to drive them crazy. It is usually husbands being indifferent, failing to communicate and demonstrating other forms of neglect."

Harley listed several comments from women about why their relationship went wrong:

"My husband is no longer my friend."

"The only time he pays attention to me is when he wants sex."

"We're like ships passing in the night; he goes his way and I go mine . . . My husband has become a stranger to me; I don't even know who he is anymore."

There are many more, but at the core of hearts breaking is a breakdown in communication.

In a terrific book called *For Men Only*, Shaunti and Jeff Feldhahn discussed how women like to talk about relationships. When a man says, "I do," the woman often wants to know, "Do you?"

As in, "Do you still love me?"

Or as the authors wrote, "When latent insecurity is triggered, (women) are often occupied with getting the relationship back on track."

If the Cleveland Browns had scouted and recruited as well as I did with Roberta, they'd be playing for a title every year. But I can still mess up our relationship—and not just through addictions, adultery or abuse. Those obviously are major issues that often do (and should) lead to divorce.

But too many men are like some college coaches. When the coaches are recruiting a prospect, they shower the player with attention: cards, texts, emails and long phone conversations. Once the kid is in the program, it's "Shut up and get to work."

Once some men close the deal by marrying their wives, it's like we say, "OK, let's shut up and get to work."

Or as Stephen Arterburn, Fred Stoeker and Mike Yorkey

wrote in *Every Man's Marriage*: "After marriage, (the man) sees the bride as someone to look after him. Having conquered this frontier called love, we turn the relationship over to our wives and crawl back into our Conestoga wagon for a nap."

Or in my case, I saddled up and became obsessed with the next stage of my career. I was like the coach who has signed one recruit and now is on to other prospects for next year's class.

In *Every Man's Marriage*, the authors also wrote: "We can easily be satisfied with a 'business partner' relationship in marriage as long as there's peace and enough sex."

When I read that, I felt a jolt. Roberta and I spent too much time in the first 20 years of our marriage in that setup. There were no catastrophic problems, just a lot of drifting and discussing about who is doing what that day. I still have to battle to make sure that our marriage doesn't disintegrate into keeping each other's schedules straight.

Down deep, many men want to do relationships better, but they don't know how. Even reading parts of the books mentioned here would make a significant difference in the relationships, but most men would rather drink battery acid than read a book on how to relate to women.

It's sad but true.

But they may be willing to look at a list. So based on a consultation with my wife, here are tips for guys who may not only want to stay married, but also want to get along better with women. Keep in mind these are general guidelines; there will always be exceptions.

1. Don't try to fix her problem, just listen. This seems to be No. 1 for most women. They want us to reassure them, to make them feel important by actually listening to them talk. We don't do it while reading the paper, playing on the computer or watching a ball game at the same time.

2. Understand that conversation is a form of sex. For women, conversation is a connection, as is sex. Part of the reason some of our wives fell in love with us is that we paid attention to what they

had to say. We cared about what they thought. If you want more and better sex, start with more and better conversation.

3. Don't tell her what to do. Women don't think like us. They don't act like us. Often, they don't understand why we fail to value relationships the way they do. Even if this is yet another discussion of her mother, her sister, the kids. And, yes, it's the same stuff over and over. Well, we still have to listen. Keep the advice to yourself, unless she asks.

4. Listen before you say, "Can I make a suggestion?" Too often, I jump in to cut off the conversation and give some advice that Roberta has never asked for.

5. Keep the conversation going. I've written in the past that conversation to women is like sex to men. Some women have disagreed, but most who expressed opinions thought I was at least on the right road. They weren't dismissing sex. They like it. They just want more conversations besides, "What are the kids doing this weekend?" and "Did we pay the electric bill?"

6. Expect problems (especially money and sex) when communication falls apart. Yes, I'm pounding away at the communication theme because it's something that most men avoid. To many of us, communication is, "What are you doing today? Here's what I'm doing today. What's for dinner? Do we have enough money for (fill in the blank)?"

7. Hug her. Most women like nonsexual hugging. Remember when holding her hand was a big deal? Or putting your arm around her? She longs for that, even if you've been married since the War of 1812. Hold her hand when walking together. Sit close when possible.

8. Give love, get respect. The New Testament book of Ephesians says in 5:33: "Each one of you also must love his wife as he loves himself, and the wife must respect her husband." Women want our love; we want their respect. It is more complicated than it sounds. An excellent book on this topic is *Love & Respect*, by Emerson Eggerichs.

9. "Overwhelmed" can mean a lot of things. She may be tired.

She may feel as if she is failing. She may feel like she isn't getting anything done, or that she has too much to do. When a woman tells you that she's overwhelmed, what she usually wants is not advice—it's a hug and reassurance that you love her.

10. "Overwhelmed" also can mean, "Help me!" When I have mentioned the "overwhelmed" idea to some women, they countered with, "We don't just need to be hugged and told we're doing a good job, we need HELP!" So ask how you can help. And be open to helping. Take on some chores.

11. Compliment her. It could be something she wears. It could be how she keeps the house. It could be the respect she has earned on the job. It could be almost anything positive; just take a minute to look for it and tell her.

12. Never criticize her in public. And *never* means *never*. Praise her to friends and family members. Make a point to introduce her to people who come up to you. Tell them how much you appreciate her . . . and do it with her standing there.

13. Be careful when you are around people who criticize the women in their lives. This can poison your relationship. Friends who are upset with their relationships can cause you to become more critical of the women around you.

14. Find out her "love language" and speak it. This is an interesting concept put forth in a terrific book by Gary Chapman called *The 5 Love Languages*. For my wife, it's spending time with her. Do at least look at this book.

15. Pray out loud with her. It doesn't matter if you feel uncomfortable. If you claim to be a man of faith, then show it. If you can get naked with this woman, then you can pray with her. I know that I dwell on praying with the woman in your life in other areas of this book, but it's critical—not optional.

28

What Women Need to Know

When my wife and I became serious about our faith—and marriage—in the late 1990s, we began to read books on relationships together.

Roberta and I would read them out loud, a few pages at a time. Sometimes we would read a chapter separately, underline something we found interesting, and talk about it.

I know, it sounds like work.

I also know a lot of people who are divorced. Talk about agony and regret with consequences lasting for years, even decades.

Divorce can be compared to someone dropping a hand grenade into your trunk. It seems as if you'll never put the pieces of your car back together.

Or, in this case, your life.

Yes, there are "no-fault" divorces, but all of them still bring pain.

So if you can make a marriage work, then be willing to work at it.

A good place to start is the book *The 5 Love Languages* by Gary Chapman. You can rate them 1-to-5, most to least important.

Here's his list, with my quick scouting report:

1. Words of Affirmation: Some people need to hear praise often . . . and really struggle with criticism.

2. Quality Time: Spending time alone, and away from others. This was No. 1 on our list.

3. Receiving Gifts: What it says.

4. Acts of Service: Doing favors for the other. Find out what the other person wants done, and do it.

5. Physical Touch: This is everything from non-sexual hugs and kisses to sexual intimacy.

I can say that after discussing No. 5, I became more intentional about non-sexual touch, and my wife became even more aware of the importance of sex in our relationship. But this happens only if you talk about it.

You can read more about the love languages at:

www.5lovelanguages.com

I did ask Roberta for help on this list to help women relate to men:

1. "Don't expect him to think like you do," my wife wrote. "Women tend to be more complicated; men are more simple and direct. If you want him to do something for you, *tell* him. Don't expect him to see it for himself. Don't expect him to do something just because you'd do it if you were in his place."

I know some women who think that can't be true, or that being called simple . . . or literal . . . would insult men.

While most of us men hate to read instructions, we do like clear and concise guidelines on what to do. I mentioned this comment to a female psychiatrist, and she said, "Men are very simple compared to women."

It was not meant to be a criticism—just a fact. I know her husband. They've been married forever, and seem to be solid. They not only accept their differences, but they also expect to be different.

2. There are times each day when a man can be very content just to exist.

You ask him, "What are you thinking?"

He says, "Nothing."

You can't believe it. But that's what he means—nothing. He's not thinking of anything. He's like a computer that is turned off. The screen is dark, but it is plugged in . . . recharging. He is glad to shut down his brain, and maybe stare at the newspaper or TV.

3. After games, there is a "cooling-off period" when no one is allowed in the dressing room. It's also time for players to relax. When most men come home from work, they want a cooling-off period. They don't want to hear everything that happened during your day, or all that you need done. Make a deal on a time frame— perhaps 30 minutes—and then ask him to listen or promise to help you.

4. My wife wrote this as a tip: "Don't expect him to be like a girlfriend and want to discuss things to death."

That's not an excuse for a guy to shut down, but after 20 to 30 minutes most men are usually finished with a subject.

5. Your spouse can be your best friend, but not your *only* good friend. You need others. Women need women friends. Men need men friends. After a while, in too many marriages, outside friend-ships disappear. That leads to problems, especially if one partner wants to have other friends.

6. In the movie *Jerry Maguire*, Tom Cruise romances a wom-an by saying, "You complete me."

No man can complete you. In our marriage, it was becom-ing serious about our Christianity that began to fill in the gaps. But there will always be gaps in a relationship. As with life, there aren't many days when it's ideal.

7. Your partner can't be responsible for your happiness. He can't make everything in your life right. He can't fill every need. In a healthy relationship, both parties take responsibility for their own emotional health.

8. If he asks you, "What is wrong?" don't answer with some-thing like, "If you loved me, you'd know." Just tell him. Be glad he asked. Sometimes we don't even notice that something is wrong with our partners.

9. If something *is* wrong, go to him. Tell him. Ask, "When is a good time for us to talk?" If he says, "Later," ask him, "When? Let's pick a time. We do need to talk." Don't keep a long list, stuffing down all the frustrations—and then explode. Men feel overwhelmed in those situations because so many things are coming at them at once, they can't process it all.

10. Help him prioritize. If you need him to do several things, say, "These two are the most important. We need them done today." Don't expect him to know your priority list.

11. When you ask him to do the laundry or clean up, and he doesn't do it *exactly* as you'd do it, don't criticize him. Odds are you do things that aren't *exactly* the way he'd have done them, but he's OK with that.

12. Men can be strange. They'll sit around and call out the names of old ballplayers. They may cry when finding old baseball cards, or at the scene in the movie *Field of Dreams* when the father and son play catch. But they probably won't remember much about your first date, or some things from your past that you consider important.

13. Although some women told me I was wrong when I said that most women consider conversation to be like sex for men, many women agreed. So guess what is like sex for most men? That's right, sex. As my wife wrote: "Never use sex as a weapon." Most couples need a sincere discussion on this topic.

PEOPLE, FAITH AND PAIN

I have a little bit of wisdom that I carry in my wallet as a reminder. It is from one of your columns about forgiveness: "When you forgive, you in no way change the past, but you sure do change the future!"

—Mary Lu Kagler, Hudson

29

Is That You, God?

People who say they always hear God's voice make me a little nervous.

I'm talking about God's *voice,* as opposed to "hearing something from God."

You can read a chapter from the book of Proverbs every day and learn something from God. It's a good idea to do that, match it to the calendar. I'm writing this on the 15th of the month. So I turn to Chapter 15 of the book of Proverbs.

No. 1 is: "A gentle answer turns away wrath, but a harsh word stirs up anger."

That is hearing something "from God."

No. 33 (the last Proverb of Chapter 15) reads: "The fear of the Lord teaches a man wisdom, and humility comes before honor."

There are a lot of lessons in both of these proverbs.

That's different from directly hearing the voice of God, a voice out of nowhere.

But it does happen, or at least it has several times in my life.

Just not often.

The most significant time was in 1998. I had become serious about my faith about six months earlier. My father was nearly five years into dealing with a major stroke that caused him to be disabled.

Couldn't walk.

Couldn't talk.

Couldn't move his right hand.

Couldn't move his right leg.

Couldn't read, couldn't write.

The list of what the stroke stole from him could go on, but you get the point. He had been in and out of the hospital with everything from a broken hip to an irregular heartbeat.

It was Feb. 5, 1998. I had spent 10 days with my father in Sarasota, Fla., where he lived. Part of that time he was in the hospital, but then I brought him home. The doctors were just warehousing him, not really treating anything. I knew he'd be happier at home, and we could hook up some oxygen.

His condition appeared to stabilize. He had an outstanding caretaker named Karen Cochran, who had been with him since the stroke. She took over, and I knew he was in good hands.

So I went home to Akron.

On Feb. 5, I was to drive to Detroit, where I'd catch a flight to Japan.

That's right, Japan.

I was assigned to cover the Winter Olympics . . . in Japan. The *Akron Beacon Journal*, the newspaper where I worked at the time, had paid about $2,500 for the flight and a place for me to stay during the Olympics. I had a bad feeling about taking the trip because of my father's condition, but nothing was different. He had been dealing with the stroke and heart issues for a long time.

Yes, his condition was serious, but no worse than it had been for months.

Before beginning my drive to Detroit, I called Karen. She said my father wasn't in great shape, but not much had changed since I had left a few days earlier. She didn't think anything life threatening was about to happen.

Just more of the same.

That's also what I saw in the future . . . more months of more of the same . . . waiting for him to die, watching him lose a little bit of his life each week.

As I was driving to the Detroit airport—it was cheaper to fly to Japan from Detroit than from Akron or Cleveland—I was silently praying about my father's situation.

And then I heard a clear voice: *Don't go.*

At first I thought little of it. I went back to thinking and praying about my father. And I heard the voice again: *Don't go.*

I thought, "God, is that you?"

I heard nothing else, but the words lingered in my head: *Don't go.*

I pulled into a truck stop in Toledo. I called Karen again. She said my father was up and eating breakfast. No change.

I hung up, closed my eyes and prayed silently: "God, now what?"

I heard the voice one more time: *Don't go.*

I called my boss at the *Beacon Journal.* I told him that I didn't think I should go to the Olympics.

He asked, "Is your dad back in the hospital?"

I said, "No, he's still at home."

He asked, "Has anything changed?"

I said, "Not really. I just don't feel good about going to Japan."

He paused and then said, "Look, just don't go."

I said that I'd pay the paper for the ticket, the Olympic housing . . . He stopped me and said, "We'll worry about that later. Just go home."

So I did.

And nothing happened that day.

Before going to bed, I called my father's home once more, and Karen said he was OK. I spoke briefly with my dad, who couldn't talk other than to say "Man . . . man" and a few grunts. But that had been his pattern since the stroke.

I went to bed.

At 4 a.m. the phone rang. It was my brother, who lived near my father in Sarasota.

"Dad died," he said. "I'm here with the paramedics."

I told him that I'd be on the first flight to Florida. After hanging up, I realized that I would have been just arriving at the Olympic village in Japan. And my wife would have been trying to track me down. And I would have been panicking about returning to Florida to help with the funeral.

I had tears in my eyes as I silently thanked God for clearly telling me . . . *Don't go.*

I also thanked God for the editor of the *Beacon Journal,* Glenn Guzzo, who had told me to stay home.

Maybe some people hear God's voice about everything . . . some make it sound as if God talks to them in a William Faulkner sentence, as in the one that Faulkner wrote in *Absalom, Absalom!* It's thought to be the longest sentence in the history of the English language: 1,288 words.

And all of it grammatically correct.

Most of us would feel incredibly blessed to hear 1,288 words directly from God in our entire lives.

Consider Psalm 46:10: "Be still, and know that I am God."

That's because it's difficult to hear God's voice in our cluttered, noisy world. And it's because I often talk to God in my prayers but don't take time to listen. It's because I don't think God wastes words or time on long messages.

Most of the messages we get from God are similar to the words I received: *Don't go.*

I've also heard: *Call this person.*

And sometimes when I'm talking: *Shut up, already.*

Often God gives us "leadings," a sense of some type of action. Or we feel guilty when we mess up. Or we feel the need to apologize to someone.

Yes, God still speaks to us.

Taking time to listen is the hard part.

30

Who Wants No for an Answer?

When I was in my 20s, I wanted to write best sellers and sell them to movie producers. I didn't pray much back then, but I probably did tell God about my million-dollar dreams.

Thirty years later I'm glad those prayers were ignored. Back then I wasn't ready for success as a writer or a person. I could have become a walking testament to what happens when someone gets too much, too soon. I already was battling a bulging ego because I was covering baseball for the *Plain Dealer*—my hometown paper—at the age of 24. I was one of the youngest baseball writers in the country, and I also thought I was one of the best.

I was not.

Pretty good, but not in the class as Peter Gammons, Jayson Stark and others who were on the beat in the early 1980s.

I also believed that because I had published a few sports books (none of which sold very well), I could become a novelist.

Trying to write fiction and piling up more than 1,000 manuscript pages was excellent experience, primarily because I didn't sell a single word from those projects.

We can learn more from failure than from some successes.

My professional life had been much too easy. Looking back, I see a young sportswriter who had too many opinions on things of which he knew little. And also a writer who needed to be told, "Not everything pounded out of your keyboard is like Moses coming down with God's tablets from Mt. Sinai."

Some prayers are best unanswered, or at least not answered according to our wishes or on our timetable.

Had my hopes and dreams of huge paychecks from my writing become reality, it wouldn't have been a shock if I had lost my marriage. Most people who have too much, too soon tend to fall into that trap. There is a reason the rich and famous tend to change spouses about as often as they trade in their luxury vehicles: A new model is enticing.

So a million-dollar payday in my 20s would have been way too much, too soon.

I'm grateful that God said no to that prayer, especially since I prayed so little and had almost zero interest in having a real relationship with God that would have required me to make any significant changes in my life.

It was only after several years of pain and frustration that I began to move in the direction that God wanted me to go.

So when it came to making me a best-selling author, God's answer was . . . *No.*

But in some cases, the answer is . . . *Not yet.*

Marshall Brandon was sure God was calling him to a career in prison ministry as a paid chaplain. But it took years to get that job. Instead he ministered as a part-time volunteer while working full time at Ohio Edison.

"Eleven years after I was sure God wanted me in ministry, I was hired at the Haven of Rest [Akron's city mission]," Brandon said.

He says those extra 11 years in the workplace gave him a better idea of what people deal with each day. It also helped him put more time away from the few years that he spent in gangs and in jail as a young man. He had even toyed with being in the Black Panthers for a while.

"No one had a perfect life growing up," Brandon said. "My father was an alcoholic. But that doesn't mean I have to drink. We all make our own choices."

When Brandon decided to become a sincere Christian and sensed God pulling him into ministry, he couldn't figure out why it had taken so long. He did a lot of volunteer ministry in jails and prisons. It was almost as if his dedication was being tested.

"On my job at Ohio Edison, I also helped point at least a dozen co-workers to the Lord in that time," Brandon said. "But I admit I got tired of all the waiting. I was being trained while waiting but didn't realize it."

Brandon is now a full-time minister. While the waiting was frustrating, it also was God's way of driving out some of the anger that he had carried from his childhood to being a soldier in Vietnam to life on the streets. Those experiences became an asset only when he was able to view them through mature eyes and a Biblical world view based on forgiveness.

The hard truth is there are occasions when the best answer to our prayers is that awful four-letter word: WAIT.

Some of us prayed to be married to a certain person, but the relationship collapsed before anyone said, "I do." Now we are thankful because that marriage would have meant misery. But most of us remember only the painful prayers that weren't answered our way:

The healing that didn't come.

The jobs that were lost and never replaced with something as good.

The children who got in trouble and stayed in trouble.

Many of us have wondered, "Where was God when I prayed?"

But we also can have amnesia about the times that we prayed for the wrong things.

"We don't always know how to pray for what is best for us," said the Rev. Bill Buckeye of Bay United Methodist Church in Bay Village. "Our view is so small, and we are so impatient."

Buckeye added that it's like the phone commercial in which someone delivers what they think is a news flash only to be told,

"'That's so 17 seconds ago.' Now 17 seconds is too long to wait."

While in high school, I wanted to attend college in New England. I didn't have the grades for the Ivy League or the cash for a school such as Boston College.

So I stayed in Northeast Ohio and went to Hiram College for a year, just long enough to meet Roberta. We've been married since 1977.

When financial problems hit, I transferred to Cleveland State University, where I ended up working part time for the old *Cleveland Press*. That started my writing career.

God's plan was a lot better than mine, even if it meant my name didn't appear on the best-seller list.

Father Damian Ference teaches philosophy at Borromeo Catholic Seminary. His mother was diagnosed with breast cancer when he was 10. Over the next 15 years she would have ovarian cancer, liver cancer and a second round of breast cancer.

He often prayed for God to cure her.

The cure never came.

"I didn't see it that way, but God was using my mother's illness to train me," said Ference said. "I now can go into any hospital, any hospice, any emergency room, and be with any family coping with life-and-death issues. I know what it's like for the family."

Ference said his mother died one year before he was ordained a priest.

"I wanted her to be there for my ordination," he said. "At the end she was down to 78 pounds. She was ready to go, at peace with God. My faith grew just watching her through all this—even though it was hard because she had dealt with a lot of pain in her life."

None of this means we should skip prayer or be afraid to pray for something.

"But it is humbling," Buckeye said. "There just is so much we don't know about how God works, or what we really need in our lives."

31

Do You Want to Get Well?

They couldn't stay sober for a month.

That's what Dan Page thought after learning that three of his friends from the drug/alcohol rehabilitation center where they all were treated were back drinking and/or on drugs.

Page wasn't feeling self-righteous about it, just sad. Thirty days of intense rehabilitation and he was the only one from his group of four who was still sober.

"I had never been in rehab before, but I found out that most people had to go two or three times," he said. "Some people in the program knew it as well as those who were teaching and leading it."

Knew it but couldn't do it.

Or didn't want to do it.

"One of my main counselors was a tattooed lady named Connie," Page said. "She had been sober for 30 years. She told me over and over, 'Relapse is optional.' That stuck with me."

Page is approaching his seventh year of sobriety. He is the pastor of Cornerstone Community Church in Stow. For years, he drank at home, and few people outside his family knew about it. He drank vodka because it was harder to detect than other liquor.

"When I drank, I drank to get drunk," he said. "I'd get depressed about how things were going with me personally and at the church, and I'd choose to drink."

All that did was make him angrier and more frustrated.

"I knew it was hard on my family," Page said. "I felt the shame, the guilt and the fear of getting caught. I knew it was wrong."

But in the end he didn't care. Or, at least he didn't care enough to stop drinking. It was only when his wife and children left and called other members of his family to tell them about his drinking that Page knew it was serious.

"We had what amounted to a family intervention," he said. "Then I went to Laurelwood [in Willoughby]. I went through the feeling that I had blown it so bad that my wife and kids would hate me, and the church would get rid of me. After all, I was living a lie."

Cornerstone was a church of about 80 regulars, with Page as the only full-time staff member when he entered rehabilitation. And the church decided to stay with him, as long as he joined an accountability group and stayed sober.

"Many of my pastor friends are blown away by the kindness the church showed me," he said. "When I first came out, I had great help from pastors Knute Larson and Jim Colledge, among others. Basically, the message was if I was caught in one lie, it was over."

Page still talks on a regular basis with three other men whose names he keeps private. Yes, it's about staying sober. But much of the talk and prayer are about facing things in their lives, not stacking up the issues and anger.

"I could see God's hand in all of this," he said. "When I got out of rehab, my wife and kids were back at home. The church was willing to give me another chance. But I also knew that I couldn't blow it. I had a bad white-knuckle period maybe six months into sobriety, but I haven't had many since."

Page is 53. He regrets "all the time and money I wasted, and all the pain that I caused."

But he has asked forgiveness from God and from those he hurt. Some people forgave him, and relationships were restored; others remain distant. There is satisfaction in being sober, but Page battles to make his marriage better, his money last longer and his church grow.

Walking away from addictive behavior doesn't lead to a stroll down life's Easy Street.

Many of the same problems that led to drinking remain after a person stops. Page still gets discouraged, but he doesn't get drunk. He often gets help from close friends he can talk to and pray with.

"I often ask, 'Aren't you just really tired of this?'" Page said. "It really is true that when you are sick and tired of being sick and tired, then you really are ready to change."

32

Suicide and Survival

A reader told me about receiving an email from his adult son. Sent a day before the father read it, the email simply said: "I just want you to know that I love you."

By the time the dad saw the email, his son had already committed suicide. "If only I had read it earlier," the reader said. "I can't remember the last time that he told me that he loved me."

It's doubtful that seeing the email earlier would have made any difference, as the message offered no hint of suicide.

That's something everyone needs to remember.

A few years ago a high school coach told me about trying to help a former player. The young man was battling depression but seemed to have it under control. He had enrolled in junior college and was finishing his first year with decent grades. He wanted to join the military. The coach thought it was a great idea, and they were discussing which branch.

Then the young man hanged himself in his mother's basement.

"I never saw that coming," the coach told me. "Maybe if I had talked to him more, listened better."

Probably not.

The coach probably would not have been able to stop it, especially since the young man had a history of depression.

"Most people who commit suicide have been dealing with emotional problems for a long time," said Kevin James, pastor of New Community Bible Fellowship in Cleveland Heights. "I have a friend whose son committed suicide. There is nothing that man could have done or said to change what happened, but he still deals with grief and some guilt."

Faith leaders seldom talk about suicide.

"It's truly a harrowing subject," said Bishop Joey Johnson of Akron's House of the Lord. "It's not like someone died of cancer, or even in a car accident. Some people don't know what to say, and they don't even want to think about it."

Jonathan Schaeffer, pastor of Grace Church in Middleburg Heights, said: "When someone tells me about a suicide in the family, the first thing I do is tell them that my heart aches for them. I then say that I can't imagine how they feel, but I am so sorry. Then I keep quiet and see what the person wants to say."

*   *   *

I spoke with former NFL quarterback Eric Hipple about this subject, not long after Denver Broncos wide receiver Kenny McKinley died when he shot himself. It seemed shocking, a 23-year-old special teams player making $395,000. His 2-year-old son had come to visit only 10 days before McKinley's death.

"He just had his second knee injury," Hipple said. "There had to be fear that he might never play again. There could have been other issues. Suicide often comes down to dealing with a loss, and a fear of becoming a burden."

Hipple played for the Detroit Lions in the 1980s. He's also the outreach coordinator for the University of Michigan Depression Center, where he specializes in suicide prevention and helping families and friends of people who have committed suicide.

This subject is not just academic to Hipple; it's personal.

His 15-year-old son committed suicide, which is why he is

dedicated to talking and teaching about a subject so few want to discuss.

"I can look back now and see things in Steven's life where he was battling depression," Hipple said, "but I didn't know then what I do now. I didn't see it coming."

Over and over again friends and family members say that same thing: "I didn't see it coming."

That's because it's hard to imagine someone actually committing suicide.

Thinking about it . . . yes.

Many of us have had periods where we may have felt the world or our families would be better off without us . . . or when we thought no one would miss us if we suddenly disappeared.

Live long enough, and most of us will know a person who commits suicide. Hipple said people usually handle the suicide of someone close to them in three ways:

1. Denial: They pretend it was an accident or a prank that went terribly wrong.

2. Guilt and Anger. They beat themselves up for not having seen it coming. Or they blame the schools, the doctors, or someone else for not having spotted the problem.

3. Resignation: They aren't surprised. The person had been suffering with mental illness for years.

Hipple said the families and friends of people who commit suicide need help, especially from others who have been through the same ordeal. No one really wants to talk about this.

"My way of coping was guilt and anger," Hipple said. "I was involved with him as a dad, but I still thought I could have been a better father."

Hipple went through months of drinking and drug use. He filed for bankruptcy. He was arrested for drunk driving after driving home from the Silverdome following a Monday night Detroit Lions game—and did 58 days in the Oakland County Jail. It was a long journey from the day in 2000 when his son killed himself with a shotgun to the time in jail to enrolling at the University of Michigan to being awarded the 2008 Lifetime Achievement Award by the American Foundation for Suicide Prevention.

At least 80 percent of suicides happen because the person is suffering from mental illness, Hipple said. Hipple's son was a star on the freshman high school basketball team. But late in the season he began to isolate himself. He stopped working in school and his grades slipped.

"He had classic signs of depression," Hipple said, "but I didn't know it."

Over and over he told himself that he should have seen it coming.

"The only reason I didn't commit suicide after my son died is I knew how hard it was on everyone around him," Hipple said. "Otherwise, I think I would have done it. I was that depressed."

Now Hipple knows that mental illness runs in his family—one member had schizophrenia, another was bipolar. Hipple realizes that he showed many of the same symptoms of depression as his son. It's so much easier to talk about a family member who died of cancer, or who was a bystander killed by a criminal.

Those who have a family member who committed suicide, Hipple said, need to be especially on guard "because studies show they are six times more likely to attempt suicide."

Why?

"Because the pain of suicide is just so great," Hipple said. "It's hard to describe unless you have been close to someone who did commit suicide. That's why those of us who have been through this need to help each other. And please, if you think about suicide, go see a psychologist or a doctor. Get some treatment. Don't wait."

*   *   *

Father Walt Jenne of St. Basil the Great Church in Brecksville said that when someone calls him about losing a family member or a friend to suicide, "I usually go see the person. I am there just to sit with them, to listen, to be there. I'll pray with them if they want. It's so hard, because they often want a rational explanation for what is an irrational act."

Some who commit suicide have stopped taking their medication. They may be addicted to drugs or alcohol. Depression probably is a factor.

Families need to remember this, according to Bishop Joey Johnson.

"A person's choice is a person's choice," he said. "We either accept it or we don't. If we don't accept it, nothing changes for the person who died—but we become angry and bitter. If we can accept the fact that the person saw no other way out, then we can deal with the guilt or anger that we feel."

Pastor Jonathan Schaeffer said his church has hosted a Survivors of Suicide support group. Another excellent resource is the National Alliance on Mental Illness. Johnson said that grief recovery programs at his and other churches can help.

"If someone close to you committed suicide, you need to realize that you'll need to work through this and you can't do it yourself," Johnson said. "And it will take a long time."

Schaeffer sometimes recites Psalm 34:18 to survivors of suicide: "The Lord is close to the brokenhearted and saves those who are crushed in spirit."

Their hearts often are shattered. Survivors can feel abandoned, rejected and resentful that they are left to clean up all the emotional and financial fallout.

Can those who commit suicide go to heaven? All four pastors that I interviewed think it's possible.

"God sent His son to save us," Jenne said. "Some people want to know why God would let this happen. God gives us free will. But I also believe in a very compassionate God who understands what that person is going through."

*   *   *

I received this email from Francis DeChant, who wanted her story told because so many parents who lose children to suicide beat themselves up:

> I have five children. I lost one, a son, my firstborn, to death by suicide. That was 30 years ago. I will never forget him or the long . . . long . . . long effort to help him overcome learning disabilities and other problems. It was a battle we lost. Did my son's life and tragic departure mean that I am never allowed to experience happiness myself? Surely his final condition was as far from happiness as eternity is from time.
>
> Does that mean I have no right to shape for myself an existence that is often touched by joy, is deeply satisfying, and holds many humorous moments? In my middle 70s, I travel to spend time I relish with my surviving children, their families and my grandchildren. I work teaching preschool gymnastics. I have many friends, volunteer to help inner-city children improve their reading skills. I'm deeply committed to my faith community. I wake up every morning glad to welcome a new day.
>
> I'm not alone. Nearly every large family I know has a difficult or troubled child. Some of the small ones do, too. Among my friends are moms who support and advocate for their mentally ill children along with their fathers. I wonder if we are not the real majority, able to rebuild lives once or even now devastated by illness, disabilities and death of our children.

Her advice is simple: Keep on living and loving those near us.

- *33* -

Forgiveness at a Funeral

The brother and sister had barely spoken for more than 50 years.

By the time they were in their 90s, the sister had severe Alzheimer's disease and was living in a long-term-care facility. While her brother didn't live in the same town, he sometimes visited the city where the facility was located—but he never visited his sister.

Then she died. Let's call her Sarah.

Enter my friend, whom we'll call David.

Sarah was David's mother. The only son in the family, David was making arrangements for her funeral at a local temple. He called his uncle, who didn't seem especially interested in the news of Sarah's death.

Still, David told his uncle that the family would love to have him at the service, or at least later at the family dinner.

David said he's not even sure what had caused the family problems.

"I think it had to do with the fact that my father didn't like the woman who my uncle married," he said.

That was more than 50 years ago.

David had been praying that his uncle would come to the fu-

neral. He even asked the rabbi to wait 10 minutes after the scheduled start of the service, just in case the uncle was late.

But he did not show up.

Later that night David called his uncle and said, "We missed
you at the service."

The uncle simply said, "Thanks," before slamming down the
phone.

David couldn't sleep because he was so angry.

"I wanted him to know how he'd hurt the family," David said.
"But I thought about him being 90. I thought how he was the
only member of that generation left in our family."

Early the next morning David wrote his uncle an email saying the service for Sarah had gone well, mentioning some of the
people who had attended.

He added: "We really missed you. We want to see you soon.
I want you to know that no matter what, my door will always be
open to you."

David said it took a lot of prayer to take that extra forgiving
step.

"The man did hang up on me," he said.

A few hours after David sent the email, there was a reply.

"I got the warmest response," David said. "My uncle wrote all
these memories of growing up with my mother. He wrote some
nice things about some other members of the family. He said he
planned to visit."

The uncle didn't write a word about what had led to the family mess or express any anger. David forwarded the email to other
family members, who also wrote to the uncle. More kindness
flowed.

David's 20-something son set up a visit with the uncle, so they
could work on putting together a family tree.

"I couldn't believe how it all changed," David told me. "My
uncle explained there would have been too much family baggage
had he gone to the funeral."

Sometimes forgiveness and reconciliation demand lots of patience and one more painful step.

"I'm glad this has happened," said David, "but it makes you wonder why it couldn't happen earlier while my mother was still alive."

I shared David's story with Rabbi Stephen Grundfast of Akron's Beth El Congregation. The rabbi nodded and said with a sigh, "I've heard it before. People have been fighting for so long, they don't even know why. It takes one person, as [David] did, who keeps reaching out and does the healing."

David put Leviticus 19:18 into practice: "Do not seek revenge or bear a grudge against one of your people, but love your neighbor as yourself. I am the Lord."

"I just let it go and let my uncle know we loved him," David said. "I'm still amazed by what happened after that."

- 34 -

The New Normal

A friend recently stopped by the cemetery where his 32-year-old daughter-in-law is buried.

"This just isn't right," he said to himself, thinking about her death from cancer and how she left behind a 3-year-old son and a husband.

"I know that God never gives us more than we can handle," he told me, his voice trailing off.

Actually, the Bible doesn't say anything directly about God giving you only what you can handle.

As reader Tom Vicarel emailed, "I've heard that many times, but it's a misquote of 1 Corinthians 10:13."

That passage reads: "And God is faithful; he will not let you be tempted beyond what you can bear."

Temptation is one thing; tragedy is another.

"There are times when it seems we are getting more than we can handle," said Paul Sartarelli, pastor at The Chapel in Akron. He told about his wife delivering their daughter prematurely when he first entered the ministry. His wife was at the Cleveland Clinic. His daughter was at Akron Children's Hospital. And Sartarelli was trying to hold down a new job while traveling between the hospitals.

"I had people tell me that God must have great things in store for me because of all I was going through," Sartarelli said. "I said that there had to be a better way to prepare me than this, because it was about ready to kill me."

Especially the worry.

"As if things weren't bad enough, I was creating even worse scenarios in my mind," he said.

So don't throw out the "God never gives us more than we can handle" line to someone who is hurting.

"In the middle of a crisis, the last thing a person needs is a lecture," said Kevin James, pastor of New Community Bible Fellowship in Cleveland Heights. "Usually, the less said, the better. Listening never makes a situation worse."

There also is the temptation to try to explain something bad by linking it to a poor decision. When I hear that someone has cancer, the first thing I wonder is, "Did he smoke?" It's almost a relief to hear that the person has been sucking on two packs of Camels for years.

That's because it's scary to discover that someone with cancer is a marathon-running health freak who ate nothing but organic seaweed. Or to hear the story of my friend, whose daughter-in-law didn't smoke. Months later, the family remains heartbroken over her death.

A Roman Catholic saint named Teresa of Avila once said, "If this is how God treats his friends, no wonder he has so few of them!"

Historians report she spoke those words with a smile. She had lost her mother at the age of 14. She contracted malaria in her early 20s. She was unable to walk for three years and battled severe illnesses all of her life. She became a nun and started 17 convents.

But I haven't been hearing from people such as Teresa of Avila.

Instead, it's the former Mid-American Conference baseball player who graduated, spent 11 years in advertising and then was laid off. He now is going back to school for an education degree and helping to pay for it by substitute teaching.

Welcome to the new normal for so many people in crisis.

That phrase comes from investor Roger McNamee in his book to describe the changing situation in the stock market. He said in an interview with fastcompany.com that the theme is: "Forget about the Next Big Thing. The next thing is here, and it's called the New Normal. The New Normal isn't where you wait for the next boom; it's about the rest of your life."

He meant that investors have to look at the stock market in an entirely new way—and his book was published in 2004. How many new normals have we had since then? The phrase has been picked up by people in ministry, psychology and other fields to deal with those times when "life happens."

The Rev. John Loejos of St. E Premte Orthodox Church in Cleveland emailed me about a meeting with former Browns star Dante Lavelli and his wife, Joy, at Bucci's restaurant in Rocky River: "She and Dante came along with the late Herb Score [the former Tribe star and broadcaster] and his wife [Nancy]. Dante was in very frail health, and Herb was in a wheelchair. Dante was standing behind Herb's chair, holding on for support. It was sad to see them in their frail conditions, but it was a thrill to see them together."

No one in those families had imagined such a scene, or a life in which those men would not be able to lead their families.

Few pitchers threw harder than Score in the 1950s. Few receivers were faster than Lavelli.

But at the end of their lives, neither could walk on his own without help.

It seems like we're always going through a new normal, because very little stays the same. I sometimes think, "If I can get through this crisis, everything will be fine." Then something else happens, and I discover that what I once considered a crisis was really an annoyance compared with what I'm facing.

It doesn't feel normal, but it is the new reality.

During a Sunday service in 2009, Pastor Knute Larson asked people to stand for prayer if they, or someone close to them, were experiencing job problems. At least one-third of the people at The Chapel—the Akron megachurch—came to their feet.

"In any given year in every church, there are people in pain and going through trials," Larson said. "But with the economy, there are so many more, and it's so public."

Larson mentioned how he takes comfort in 2 Corinthians 12:9, where Paul asked God to take away "a thorn in the flesh" three times. God didn't, and instead answered, "My grace is sufficient, for my power is made perfect in weakness."

Some people repeat that verse several times a day as they cope with everything from chemotherapy to standing in line at the unemployment office.

The new normal? It means accepting that the old normal is gone.

In her book *A New Kind of Normal*, Carol Kent wrote about what she learned after her son was arrested on a murder charge: "We can lie down, curl up in the embryo position, quit life and die emotionally and spiritually—or with every fiber of our being, we can choose life. We can choose perseverance. We can choose gratitude."

Those are some first steps, but so is prayer . . . prayer for the power to get to the next normal, which could be better than the one today.

LAST WORDS

"Your article touched my heart and literally set me free—praise God! I had a similar experience with my Mom. I, too, had to make the final decision about her operation and then she died a few weeks later. I have talked to family and close friends and nothing quite soothed that pain, or shall I say guilt. But when you said you were forced to choose between two lousy alternatives, my burden was lifted. I thank you for sharing so intimately with your readers."

— Norma McAlpine, Garfield Heights

- 35 -

I . . . Don't . . . Know

I don't know.

When talking about faith, never be afraid to say these three words:

I

Don't

Know.

Nothing wrong with saying them slowly and quietly.

Nothing wrong with not knowing.

And there is especially nothing wrong with offering them to a hurting person.

Consider this email from David:

> Look at those innocent kids in Chardon [the accused gunman is a fellow student at their school]. There was a young girl in East Cleveland killed . . . a 20-year-old Kent State girl killed in a traffic accident. There was a baby, two years old, who walked into an open pool in Tallmadge and drowned. What did they do wrong in their lives to deserve death when they were just beginning to live? Look at the incredible pain that has been delivered to their families and friends. And it didn't matter that the Kent State girl's parents were huge supporters of a Catholic church in Ravenna either.

You can come up with your own list of tragedies by watching the news or reading the paper each day.

David continued:

> One of the biggest and strongest arguments against believing in God or a higher power is: 'How can there be a God when He lets the innocent suffer? The good die young . . . and the evil seem to prosper. It's not fair and it's not right.' I know that pastors try to explain this unexplainable. Some talk about 'look at what God sacrificed.' Some talk about God needing His 'good servant to come home.' They do their best to help us understand and deal with the pain of our loss. But in the end, two things remain: It isn't fair, and why did it happen?

Rather than start with a bit of answer to one point, I'll stay with the bigger theme:

I

Don't

Know.

I don't know why a troubled kid walks into a school and starts shooting. I don't know why some kids are killed and others are spared. I do know why some toddlers fall into swimming pools— they crawl away and have no clue where they are going. A parent can't watch a toddler every second, although you can and should take precautions to keep a child away from water.

But in the end I don't know why some drown and others are saved.

*   *   *

I can understand why David and others wonder as Asaph did in Psalm 73:3: "For I envied the arrogant when I saw the prosperity of the wicked."

Lots of bad people get away with a lot of bad stuff.

Since 1998, when I began doing weekly jail ministry, I have seen how poor decisions and lifestyles eventually catch up to most people. Drinking and drug abuse destroy bodies and entire families. Fraudulent use of credit cards leads to enormous debt, and often jail time. Divorce is common. Losing connection with (and sometimes custody of) children occurs.

As it says in Numbers 32:23: "You may be sure that your sin will find you out."

Justice may come late. It may not be as severe as we'd like it to be. But when you pile up the selfish decisions—and at the heart of sin is selfishness—the sheer weight of it will make most people pay a heavy price.

Not everyone.

Not all the time.

But people who live totally for themselves and hurt so many others—well, they usually don't get away with everything forever.

I've heard people say, "You can't legislate morality."

That's something we say when we aren't thinking deeply.

We legislate morality all the time. What are laws against stealing, murder, rape, child abuse and "crimes against persons" other than saying some acts are wrong . . . and, yes, immoral?

You can say that some people consider some acts immoral while others do not. But there really is a moral baseline in society, or the result is anarchy. And most people know and accept that.

The hard part is when things just happen . . . bad things . . . to decent people.

*   *   *

The real questions that haunt us begin with one word: *Why?*

Start with "Why do some people die in automobile accidents and others do not?"

This one hits close to home. In 1995 my wife was driving down a two-lane highway in rural North Carolina. She had just spent a month with her father, who was recovering from his third heart surgery. She was on her way home that morning when a tractor-trailer jackknifed in front of her Honda Civic and smashed into her.

I don't know why she escaped with only two broken ankles. I say "only" two fractures because I spoke with the policeman first on the scene. From the look of the Civic—a crushed can—he was positive it was a fatality. He was shocked that Roberta had only the ankle injuries.

I don't know why this happened to Roberta after she had spent a month taking care of her father and being there for her mother. How about that commandment of honoring your father and mother? She was doing that.

Then she gets whacked by a truck . . . Are you kidding me?

In the book of Job, about every three pages, Job seems to ask God, "Hey, what's the deal here? What did I do wrong?"

The answer is disturbing: not much. All the calamities weren't his fault.

My first thought after hearing of Roberta's accident was much like Job's when he heard his kids had been wiped out: "Where is God in that?"

But then I talked to the policeman and I was incredibly grateful that Roberta was alive . . . so I guess God was there, after all.

I also know of people who died in seemingly less-severe car wrecks.

Former Tribe first baseman Andre Thornton was driving on the Pennsylvania Turnpike when his car hit a patch of black ice, skidded off the road and landed in a ditch. Thornton and his young son, Andre Jr., walked away from the wreck with a few minor injuries.

Thornton's wife, Gertrude, and their 3-year-old daughter, Theresa, were instantly killed.

How does that happen?

Two are basically untouched, two die . . . in the same one-car accident.

Thornton was and remains a man of strong morals and faith, one of the really good guys in sports.

My wife survived, and you'd never guess that she had ever had ankle surgery.

Thornton's wife died. So did his daughter.

A gravel truck smashed my wife's Honda.

A small patch of ice knocked Thornton's car off the road.

I don't care where anyone went to school or what holy books they have memorized; no one has a full explanation for that.

So when people ask me where is God in these seemingly random events, I often say . . .

I

Don't

Know.

I say it slowly, and I say it with an ache in my heart and a crack in my voice.

If someone really wants to discuss the subject, I may tell that person about what a man named Fred Perkins told me years ago when I was considering Christianity. We talked about God and suffering. We talked about prayer. We talked on and off for months.

He told me about his brother who was killed in Vietnam, and how he was wounded in Vietnam. He had had other physical and business setbacks. Life had not been easy. He started a meat business, and that was a major challenge.

In the end he said, "I don't know answers for a lot of things. But I do know life is hard. You either go through it with God or without God."

Then he shrugged.

A few years later his 20-something daughter died of cancer. It appeared that she had been cured of liver cancer. For about a year, the tests came back clean. It seemed that prayers had been answered. Then the disease roared back and killed her in a few months.

What did she do wrong? Or what did her parents do wrong?

What did anyone do wrong?

Nothing.

She just died.

Through their tears and unanswered questions, Fred and his family clung to their faith. But their daughter was still dead, and the hole from the loss of her will always be in their hearts.

Not only did I think of Fred's words—"Life is hard. You either go through it with God or without God"—I saw his family live them out.

*   *   *

Which brings up another aspect of faith.

I don't know how jet planes fly, but I know they do. I have no proof that when I get on a jet that is going from Cleveland to Phoenix, it actually will go to Phoenix. I buy my ticket, I hand it to someone at the gate, and I sit where they tell me to sit.

And I wait for hours, assuming the flight will go to Phoenix.

And every time I've boarded a plane to Phoenix, it's arrived in Phoenix.

Not always on time, but it has arrived every time. And it arrives at the right place almost every time, unless diverted by weather.

If you ask me how I got there . . . how the plane took off and landed . . . why it sometimes flies at 28,000 feet and sometimes at 30,000 feet . . . you might as well ask me how a caterpillar becomes a butterfly.

I don't know that, either.

Creepy caterpillars that become fluttery butterflies are as mysterious as a couple of tons of steel whizzing through the air from Cleveland to Phoenix.

Or even those rare occasions when a jet doesn't arrive where it should . . . when it crashes.

OK, I know there are explanations for why planes go down: bad weather, mechanical malfunctions, hijackings by terrorists who fly the planes into New York's Twin Towers.

I mention the last part because on September 11, 2001, I was in the air, flying from Akron to Albany. I was scheduled to speak to a group of reporters at a newspaper in Glens Falls, N.Y. As I got off the plane and walked into the Albany airport, I saw everyone staring at television screens—just as a jet flew into the second of the Twin Towers.

Several hundred people just like me had stepped onto four different planes that day.

American Airlines Flight 11 left Boston and hit one of the towers.

United Airlines Flight 175 left Boston and hit the other tower.

American Airlines Flight 77 left Washington and crashed into the Pentagon.

United Airlines Flight 93 left Newark, and then the passengers heard about what was happening in the air. They took down the terrorists, but the plane crashed outside of Shanksville, Pa.

A total of 246 people died on those four flights within a few hours of my flights that went from Akron to Pittsburgh, and then Pittsburgh to Albany.

I walked off the plane to sunshine and a beautiful September morning in upstate New York. The other people never left those planes alive, never saw their families again. In most cases, it was hard to recover enough of their bodies for their families to recognize them.

They went up in a plane one morning . . . and that was it . . . they were gone.

I had not spent much time thinking about that morning as it applied to me personally until I began writing this essay. In fact, I had no idea the memory would come up. It was not part of my notes.

But there it is: Four planes went down. Mine did not.

There were 246 people who died on those flights, and thousands more like me who were in the air but did not die. I sincerely doubt that any of those 246 people deserved to die—compared with the rest of us who did not die.

And I'm not even including the nearly 3,000 people who died in the Twin Towers, the Pentagon and the field in Pennsylvania. What was the difference between those who died and those in the Towers and the Pentagon who were on different floors and survived?

Nothing that any of us know.

So I simply say:

I

Don't

Know.

I've been writing about faith since 2000, first at the *Akron Beacon Journal* and now at the *Plain Dealer* in Cleveland.

It's odd when readers encounter a sportswriter who also does two faith columns a month.

What makes him an expert in faith?

The answer is obvious: nothing.

Nor do I claim any expertise, other than there are times when I feel free to say: "I don't know."

I can say that I'm a Christian, that life is hard, and that I have chosen to go through it with a God who has granted me forgiveness—even if I often don't understand what is going on.

I know how God has affected my life, but I also know that Jesus never said, "Hop in my Mercedes and ride with Me."

I really hate that part of all of us needing to "carry a cross," as Jesus called life.

David's email at the beginning of this essay was about the randomness of life and death, yet he ended it by saying, "The more I see of it, the more I still believe I need faith in God to get through the day."

Like David, I sense that most of us are carrying something around as we go through life—our own crosses. Life throws some crosses on our shoulders—waking up one morning with a lump that turns out to be cancer. We build other crosses. I do it through not listening, forming opinions too quickly and allowing what I call my "inner jerk" to come out at the wrong times with people who deserve better from me.

I write for people who have been hurt, people who have doubts, people who may believe in God but are like the man in Mark 9:24 who brings his mentally and physically ill son to Jesus for a cure.

Jesus said to the man, "Everything is possible for those who believe."

The man said, "I do believe; help me overcome my unbelief."

That's me: part believer, part doubter, part searcher.

My life is better with God than without God. But I also understand why some people don't buy into the "whole God thing" as a few people have called it to me . . . and those people read my faith stories regularly.

Because it takes a certain amount of faith to get through life, even when we don't understand what life is about at that particular moment.

Acknowledgements

Lots of religious leaders have helped me over the years with these columns. You will find their names sprinkled in all the chapters.

I want to thank Janet Fillmore, a wonderful editor and friend, for her time and patience as we put together this book.

I'd also like to thank everyone at Gray & Company, Publishers: David Gray, Rob Lucas, Chris Andrikanich, Jane Lassar, Jane Wipper and Frank Lavallo, as well as Pat Fernberg for her proofreading.

Finally, thanks to Susan Goldberg, Roy Hewitt, Debra Adams-Simmons, Terry Egger and Mike Starkey, who all helped bring me back to the *Plain Dealer* in 2007. And the Janet Leach, the former editor of the *Akron Beacon Journal*, who allowed me to begin writing the faith column in 2000.

About the Author

Terry Pluto is a faith and sports columnist for *The Plain Dealer*. He has twice been honored by the Associated Press Sports Editors as the nation's top sports columnist for medium-sized newspapers. He is a nine-time winner of the Ohio Sports Writer of the Year award and has received more than 50 state and local writing awards. He has also won an Amy award for his faith writing. He and his wife, Roberta, help lead weekly prison ministry services at Summit County Jail; they also do volunteer work at Haven of Rest City Mission in Akron.

He and his wife, Roberta, help lead weekly prison ministry services at Summit County jail; they also volunteer at the Haven of Rest City Mission in Akron.